From The Bored Room
TO THE BEDROOM

Biblical Secrets On How to Stimulate Your King
From The Inside Out!

Ruby Fleurcius

From The Bored Room

To The Bedroom

Biblical Secrets On How to Stimulate Your King From The Inside Out!

Spiritually Fit Publications
581 N. Park Ave. Ste. #725
Apopka, FL 32704
321-312-0744
Ruby@RubyFleurcius.com

Published in the United States of America
ISBN: 978-0983207597
$14.95

Table of Contents

Dedication 7

Introduction 9

Chapter 1
   The Virtue 13

Chapter 2
   Essential Secrets 17

Chapter 3
   Heart of a Real Woman 27

Chapter 4
   The Room of Power 35

Chapter 5
   Room of Turmoil..39

Chapter 6
   Jezebel's Room...45

Chapter 7
   The Sparkle...51

Chapter 8
   The Leader...55

Chapter 9
   The Anointing..59

Chapter 10
   Threshing Room..65

Chapter 11
   The Cord..71

Chapter 12
   Overcoming The Trickster...75

Chapter 13
    Living Water 79

Chapter 14
    Private Room Issue 85

Chapter 15
    Drawing The Line 89

Chapter 16
    Breadcrumbs of a Woman 95

Chapter 17
    From the Bored Room 103

Chapter 18
    Her Excellency 107

Chapter 19
    The Cry 113

Chapter 20
    Rubies From Within 117

Chapter 21
    Diligence 121

Chapter 22
    The Law of Reciprocity 127

Dedication

I dedicate this book to my Lord and Savior, who has so dearly blessed me beyond all measure. Holy Spirit speak to those who have an open ear. As the deep calleth unto the deep let my Breadcrumbs speak to the hearts of those who they are designed to reach. For it is You O'Lord, that kept me; it was You O'Lord that left the Breadcrumbs for me leading the way, for it was You O'Lord that enabled my Breadcrumbs to become much. It was You that dropped the Breadcrumbs of Wisdom into my Spirit. Although some may look at a Breadcrumb like it is nothing; but, Your Breadcrumbs are everything; for me—the most amazing thing about it, it is like "Manna" it never stops coming. My every need is taken care of, when I look to the right, You are there; when I look to the left, You are there. It is an honor for me to share with the world some of the Breadcrumbs that the Women of the Bible left behind for the Virtuous Women to partake. Also, I would like to take a moment to thank everyone who contributed to every Breadcrumb in my life, regardless of how big or small it was, or how good or bad, it may have been—had it not been for that positive or negative Breadcrumb, I would not be the woman that I am today. I have had a long journey through life, and it is through those Breadcrumbs that I picked up, followed, discarded, and learned from are the reasons why I am sharing this series with those who are in need of what I have to offer. I have been chosen for the Breadcrumb Journey; and if you walk with me, I will lead you with the Breadcrumbs that I have been led with. For when we fall short, Your Son is indeed the Bread of Life. In Jesus' name. Amen

Introduction

After going through many relationships, we will find that we have a sincere desire for something more than the average run-of-the-mill man. Often, we feel as if we need more than what we have or more of what we do not have. As a result, we find ourselves separated, getting a divorce, or staying in a broken relationship that has resulted in some form of physical, emotional, spiritual, or mental abuse. Now, this is your opportunity to know and understand more of what you did not know about yourself as a Real Virtuous Woman and your mate as a Man, Boy, or King. As you read this book, you will find the true value of who you are without settling for less than the best of what God has for you.

I have also found that fear is the primary culprit of unequally yoked relationships. Yes, I mean fear—fear of not finding your idea of Mr. Right, fear of not finding a man at all, the fear of having to settle down with someone with a boy mentality, a fear of not ever finding your King, or the fear of not having the perfect family. It is so amazing how fear will cause us to settle for inequality to fill the void of loneliness, insecurity, or depression. Most often, we are afraid to admit that we are NOT trusting God, so we pick up anybody to change them to appear as if they are heaven sent, and we miss out on our true King. In finding the King of your heart, it's essential that you know and understand that in which resides within you as a Real Virtuous Woman. For the most part, our King will not always be in our mate, our King may be in our child—we may have to raise a King. Therefore, it is imperative that we teach our son what to look for in a Virtuous Woman as well. In order to learn these characteristics, we must discover what some of the Women of the Bible did to snag their Kings. Actually, the Women of the Bible left us a legacy of great information that I will uncover in this book called, "From The Bored Room To The Bedroom."

In this book, you have a phenomenal reservoir to pull from that will capture the heart of Your King; however, it's your responsibility to glean as much information as possible to ensure that you gather as much as you need to make sure you learn the characteristics of a Real Virtuous Woman. You will also uncover in this book that a Virtuous Woman is first and foremost, gentle, caring, loving, and the list goes on; and, she also has an infinite knowing that's inside of her that nudges her when she has a King in front of her or whether he is a want-to-be King, a playboy, or a wolf in sheep's clothing.

Whether you are, or are not, a Virtuous Woman right now, you deserve to have a King, a good man, or a piece of a man just as much as any other woman or Virtuous Woman. This book will share valuable information with you that you are able to apply to any relationship. Even though "From The Bored Room To The Bedroom" will equip you to attract and keep your King through a systematic plan, it is not limited to just that. Now, in order to attract your King, you must clear your mind first, evaluate the situation, decide what you want, understand the circumstances, and then make a decision if need be. This will definitely save the time and energy wasted on undoing or redoing things that you should have waited on anyway. However, if you are not comfortable learning the secrets of being a Real Virtuous Woman, then this book is not for you, but if you are looking to make changes in your relationships, step-up your game, or update your prospecting process, then keep reading.

Chapter 1
The Virtue

Virtue is something that we all have an inner born desire to have; although we are born that way initially, we must be conditioned to stay that way; if not, we will naturally gravitate toward selfish behavior. For the purpose of this Book, "From The Bored Room To The Bedroom," the virtues are broken down into Breadcrumbs to give one a better understanding of how they work together to create wholeness from the inside out. This is not designed to degrade a Real Virtuous Woman; this is designed to show everyone how empowered we are when we are able to put our ego aside to accept the Bread of Life in John 6:35. If a woman has the desire to become a Real Virtuous Woman, she must be willing to understand that she cannot be selfish; she must be willing to share her Breadcrumbs of Virtue with others, while accepting people for who they are, showing a sincere concern for their well-being.

What I have found is that every woman wants to be that Proverbs 31 Woman, but somehow doesn't understand that the Proverbs 31 Woman is the last chapter of Proverbs. That means that in order to become that Proverbs 31 Woman, we cannot bypass Proverbs 1-30. We must master the previous chapters first, and the Proverbs 31 Woman is automatic—that is the true reward that Wisdom gives to women who places her first. She [wisdom] frowns upon a woman trying to reap the benefits where she has not sown. Who is She[wisdom]? In the Book of Proverbs wisdom is personified in the text as a female in nature—out of due respect, if we desire to glean from the Spirit of Wisdom according to Scripture, we must respect how it is written. As a matter of fact, if we want what She [wisdom] has to offer us, we must act like a real lady and not a thief, seducing and manipulating men into wanting something that we have not mastered. "For the lips of an adulteress drip honey and smoother than oil is her speech; but in the end, she is bitter as wormwood, Sharp as a two-edged sword." Proverbs 5:3-4. The way in which we communicate is a dead giveaway regarding our motives, and a woman with an uncontrollable mouth is a target for emotional turmoil, as well as a disruptive household. Do we think that She [wisdom] will give us the ability to love others with conditions? Do you think She [wisdom] will allow us to manipulate her prestige just to put on a show? Do we think that She [wisdom] will prize us as a virtuous woman through flattery? The answer is NO! She [wisdom] will only select those who are teachable, trainable, faithful, realistic, honest with themselves, and willing to embrace the Essence of a Virtuous Woman, for her price is far above rubies. The Virtue has some hidden Breadcrumbs that we will uncover throughout the proceeding chapters to give you a better understand the way in which she[wisdom] operates. She is no joke—she will reward you, and she will crucify you for using her in your wrongdoings. However, the wisdom that she[wisdom] holds cannot compare—she will drop Breadcrumbs in your lap that will blow your mind, guaranteed! Keep reading.

Chapter 2

Essential Secrets

It's time out for women's liberation; especially, if we find ourselves underpaid, broke, struggling, and lonely! Make no mistake about it; it's time for the Fake Wannabe Virtuous Woman to take their rightful place in society by taking a step back and relearn the ways in which the Proverbs 31 Woman designed for us to keep our families together and happy. The Proverbs 31 Woman accomplished this without having the backlash of losing the people, places, and things that she loved the most, or being labeled as bourgeois for her lavish lifestyle.

As the Essence of a Virtuous Woman fills the air, that lets us know that all of the good men are not taken—they are just waiting for her to assume her proper role by exhibiting the appropriate characteristics that charm the socks off him. It is said that behind every good man is a **Virtuous Woman** that do not buy into the 50/50 relationship—she buys into the Breadcrumb concept of the 100/100 relationship. This enables her to give 100% of herself to the development and the nurturing of oneself, her King, her family, and everything in the building of their home to promote their love, security, and freedom.

Every woman is not a Virtuous Woman, and every man is not a King; however, God lays the groundwork for the essence that we should possess. Of course, it often goes overlooked; but, now is the time for you to embrace the essence of the true Virtuous Woman that's inside of you. This type of woman knows that she is a Virtuous Woman from within, and she may not have her King at the present moment; but, she awaits his arrival, and she chooses her King very carefully. She doesn't lose hope in him because she knows that the essence of her gracefulness is designed just for him. The essence of a Real Virtuous Woman is very strategic, not problematic. She is clever, not cunning. She is wise, not a know-it-all. She is very sensual, not perverted. She is very diligent, not lazy. She is very loving, not cold-hearted. She does not play games with his emotions; however, she finds interest in the sports that he plays. She does not use alcohol, drugs, etc. to temporarily influence him; she believes in being in her right state of mind while finding out what works for her King and what does not.

Her ultimate desire is to market herself as a Virtuous Woman and not just an average woman. She is in the business of fine-tuning and taking care of herself, and then to the passion that's inside of her King or King to be. So, what should we do when the pressure of finding a King is pulling us in one direction, and the people, places, and things in our life are pulling us in a different direction? My Virtuous Woman, when we are being pulled, tugged, and pressed—that's our sign to stand still and know that our King awaits our presence. Taking our time to make wise and sound decisions will keep us on track, regardless of the type of grip that life may have on us. Thinking about what we are doing before we do it, is a great way to stay on top of our game. We have to find a way to weigh the pros and the cons before making a permanent decision regarding something or someone that's designed to be temporary. Unwise decisions will keep us running from one thing to the next, or better yet, from one person to the next; trying to find a quick fix or that quick niche that will pull us to and fro, not knowing which way to turn.

Her Essence

The essence of a true Virtuous Woman is very teachable. It's imperative that we learn—learn how to possess the Virtuous Womanship qualities. We can only do so by learning from another Virtuous Woman, and I have found that the best way to do this is to learn from the Women of the Bible. Although they may not always be referred to as a Virtuous Woman; but, they possess certain characteristics that we can learn from, and they have already laid the groundwork for our future. Therefore, we do not have to waste time undoing, redoing, overdoing, or relearning lessons that we can get the first time around. Of course, it is through their successes and failures, or their goodness and evilness that we are able to use as a preventative method of preserving or polishing up our Virtuous Womanship qualities and characteristics. We must never underestimate the substance that's provided in the Breadcrumbs of women who were designed to inspire us to the end of time. For example, Eve was our first Virtuous Woman; even though she was not referred to as a Virtuous Woman, she was a Virtuous Woman indeed. Of course, we all look at Eve as the downfall of all mankind because of her partaking of the forbidden fruit and then giving it to Adam; however, there is more value in what Eve has to offer to the Virtuous Woman of today.

Eve teaches us how to be the 1st woman. And, being a #1 woman starts with a state of mind. As we all know from Eve, we create our own destiny by the decisions we make or do not make. Our decisions may have an impact on generations to come if we do not make wise decisions to protect ourselves and our household. Therefore, bringing us to her 2nd quality that a Virtuous Woman needs to learn, and that is about our selfishness; it was out of her selfishness that she took of the fruit. We as Virtuous Women must become very cautious about our selfishness to protect our Kings and our future princes and princesses. Now, the 3rd quality, we must have eye-catching substance from within—she possessed something that Adam was not willing to give up. She catered to the boy that was inside of her King, and he was not willing to live life without having her by his side. Of course, there was a price to pay for keeping her by his side; but, that was a price that he was willing to pay. So, that's why we are here today learning from back then to better govern our right now.

The Touch
In order to touch our King, we must be willing to touch his mind, first. In so many words, we must have more to offer him than our sexuality. We must possess something that goes above and beyond what's in our bedroom; although, our sexual needs are important; however, it will lose its effectiveness if we do not put the essence of our mind power behind it. We as Virtuous Women must find ways to stimulate his mind, touch his heart, and cater to the inner child that's waiting for our attention. If we don't, we are going to lose some brownie points in that area; and trust me; this is an area that we do not want to risk losing. Once we understand the big picture of a desired King, our Virtuous Womanship

qualities should underscore his Kingdom. A Virtuous Woman's goal is to become an asset to the Kingdom and not a liability. My friend, it's hard to get rid of an asset, but it's very easy to get rid of a liability—so, we must provide some form of substance that's irreplaceable to our King. In order to find that substance, we must learn about our King; however, knowing too much information will keep us distracted. A Virtuous Woman that's too distracted is a Virtuous Woman that may turn away from her King. So, keep it simple and to the point as this brings us to the 4th quality.

Now, I hope that you are catching all the Breadcrumbs that I am leaving behind for you, because I will not point them all out—I will make you search for some; however, I do not want you to miss this one. As we all know, Adam was created from the dust and Eve was created from his rib. Being that Eve was created from his rib, she was designed to be by his side—she had the 1st insight on how to stand by her man's side. God could have created her from any other part of the body. But, He chose a rib—a Virtuous Woman is a part of what holds and keeps a King in his upright position. Stand by your King, but make sure that he is King Material before you waste your time standing beside someone or something that will bring shame to your name. So, what is King Material? A King is

1. Stable.
2. Interdependent.
3. Teachable.
4. Flexible.
5. Respectful.
6. Encouraging.
7. Positive.

8. Loving.
9. Affectionate.
10. Giving.
11. Humorous.
12. Resourceful.
13. Cooperative.
14. Open & Honest.
15. Confident.
16. Wise.
17. Sincere.
18. Supportive.
19. Interesting.
20. Loyal
21. Resourceful
22. Unselfish
23. Not Abusive
24. Protector
25. Not Lazy

You must determine if he's worth your time; because if you don't, in the long run, you will find yourself feeling sorry for him or obligated to staying in an unworthy relationship. Now, a word of caution does not waste valuable time looking for someone with these characteristics if you do not possess them as well. As a Virtuous Woman, you must possess that in which you are looking for—if you don't possess them right now, you must start working on possessing each one of these characteristics. You do not have time to redo or undo things that you have an opportunity to get right the first time around. As a matter of fact, these qualities may take a little time to manifest and develop, so don't waste time, energy and money on people, places, and things that contradict what you want and desire in your King. Just remember that every man is not going to understand that He is a King and if He does not understand or recognize that—you cannot force him to do so. If a man does not understand the difference between love and infatuation, you will find that he will run from relationship to relationship looking for something or someone that he will never understand.   Your unique way of communicating intellectually is needed, so you must pray through this process as you keep your eyes and ears open to what you are doing and what you are not doing.

When embarking upon our Virtuous Womanship, we must make a commitment to patiently persevere through all obstacles regardless of how we feel.   Actually, we must consistently think toward greatness by learning how to present ourselves strategically without becoming overbearing or desperate. We must also know and understand our purpose for doing what we are doing, as well as find out what we like and do not like in a man. Basically, we need to find out who needs what we have to offer. And, by knowing this, we are then able to create a sense of urgency or hunger for what we are offering, and that is our Virtuous Womanship.

"From The Bored Room To The Bedroom" lays the foundation for the promotion of our Virtuous Womanship without allowing her to appear as if she is desperate for a man. She presents herself as a simplistic woman that feeds others with her worthiness as she allows her King to be different from any other man. She knows how to make him feel as if he is #1 aside from God.   A real Virtuous Woman is honorable and very submissive to her King because she trusts him. With that type of trust and belief in her King, she is comfortable falling under his vision and the vision that he has for her as well as the household.

For that reason, she will never make him feel inadequate—she is grateful for him because she knows that where he is weak, she is strong and where he is strong, she is weak; therefore, creating balance and teamwork in the relationship.

We must have an idea of how we are going to treat our King whether we have him or not. Trust me; we can have the best attitude in the world, but if we lack the ability to treat him right, then we very well may fall short. Our plan of action for our Virtuous Womanship does not have to be long; actually, it's better to keep our plan simple and attainable to ensure that we are able to carry it out. Of course, with experience and perseverance, we are then able to update, enhance, or make our simple plan outstanding by knowing 7 things:

1. Know yourself and your purpose in life.
2. Know how you can make a difference.
3. Know what you want and do not want.
4. Know the impact of what you have to offer.
5. Know your competition.
6. Know how you are going to create the urgency for your Virtuous Womanship qualities.
7. Know how you are going to share what you have to generate positive results in your life.

We as women must master our Virtuous Womanship qualities by diligently getting to know what's in our heart; while making the adjustments to love, serve, and assist our King. As the competition challenges us, we must know and understand what we have to offer without becoming insecure and weak about it. We do not have to buy our King—if a man can be bought with material gain by a woman, he is not a KING, and if a woman can be bought with material gain by a man, she is not a Virtuous Woman.   A Virtuous Woman should never buy love; she must be able to share her love by doing simple things "just because" for her King that's within her budget. We must keep our Virtuous Womanship gifts as inexpensive as possible; this will prevent us from losing out before we really begin. Some things may work and some things may not, so we must keep our budgets to a minimum.

Chapter 3

Heart of a Real Woman

The Book of Esther gives us a perfect example of a Real Virtuous Woman where Esther listened to King Xerxes without judging him, talking back to him, ridiculing him, or insulting him. Let's start from the beginning; Esther was not brought up as a princess; she was brought up as an orphaned Jew that was raised by her uncle, Mordecai. She was not accustomed to living as a Virtuous Woman, and this is where she learned the basic principles on how to serve and be served under the right or wrong conditions. She won her Kings heart by unselfishly learning his likes and dislikes without judging him, as his previous wife Vashti did. Vashti was a very selfish woman who wanted her King to bow down to her when she should have been bowing down to him. In so many words, she tried to intimidate him with her beauty—intimidation is one of the quickest ways to lose the heart of your King. When a woman allows her beauty to go to her head, it will cause a man to turn away from her while he secretly looks for another woman who is more beautiful on the inside. As time continued on, Vashti talked about her King behind his back, and when you are dealing with a King, male-bashing is strictly prohibited. She also treated him very harsh, and due to her insensitivity toward her King, her harshness became common knowledge throughout the Kingdom. Therefore, based on her actions, her King decided to protect himself by closing up and rejecting her. He began to cut her off emotionally—once a man closes his heart to a woman, the relationship will begin to work against itself. Basically, He will begin to shut her down with or without just cause—he will not give her the opportunity to humiliate him when she is exhibiting reckless behavior. Besides, due to Vashti's inability to become humble and submissive, she lost her Virtuous Womanly position as well as her Crown to a woman who did not mind doing what she was not willing to do. That other woman, Esther, began to cater to the needs of that man, King Xerxes—she was soft, kind, trusting, submissive, and gentle. She was very attentive and pleasing to conversate with; her heart was open to his; she was trusting, accepting, and respectful to him, as well as showing a great interest in what he had going on in his life. Esther was everything Vashti was not, King Xerxes sought out all of the faults that Vashti had to ensure that his new Queen did not possess those same faults to ensure that she would not bring shame to his name as his previous Queen did. This happens all too often even in today's world, there are a lot of married, single, divorced, and complicated women, that have not so great attitudes that believe in humiliating their mates, with or without just cause, in public or behind closed doors. An attitudinal woman will find herself running from relationship to relationship thinking that everyone else has a problem when the actual problem lies within the depths of their very own soul. Even though we do not hear much about Vashti in the Book of Ester; her role is a cornerstone warning of how we can lose our kingdom privileges for a temporary moment of arrogant selfishness. However, it was through her selfishness that enabled Esther to take her place as a Virtuous Woman.

It has always been said that "One woman's trash is another woman's treasure," and Esther knew the value of her treasure; therefore, she prepared and beautified herself for her King—she took time out to work on her elegance, sophistication, and her body for one whole year prior to meeting King Xerxes. Esther knew that her elegance, her unselfish love, her savvy, and her willingness to make a sacrifice for others would become the key factors in winning and keeping her King. There are so many women with Real Virtuous potential that make their King the last priority because they just don't know what to do. All too often, we will find that we are keeping up with the Joneses while our King is walking right out the front door. It's sad that we want a man, but we are not willing to do what it takes to get him or keep him. We put money before our King; we put our career before our King, and we put a lot of things before our King. We do not realize that our integrity, love, and sacrifices will keep all of those things together; of course, if we put them in the proper perspective— God first, self, others, and everything else will fall into its proper place.

Get rid of the selfish agenda as Esther did—she prepared herself for her Queenship first, she got behind her King Xerxes to ensure the success of his Kingdom as well as his well-being, and she took care of others. Listen, Esther knew the value of her Breadcrumb; she knew the value of becoming his blanket of security in and out of the bedroom; she also knew that no other man could compare to her King, so she eliminated all the distractions in her life. She could not allow the opinions of others to cause her to lose out on her blessing. Even though God used her to bless other people, she knew the value of protecting her own blessing as she became the source of motivation to her King.

You are going to have to find the need in this man instead of your wants and offer him a benefit with a sense of urgency with no strings attached. However, you must do your homework—your King wants you to think about how you can serve as a benefit instead of a liability, creating lasting value that's hard to replace. He is going to need communication! You are going to have to communicate with your King, and learn how to speak his language to him. Your job is to find what stimulates this man in a conversation that causes him to listen to you on any level. As you very well know, men are VISUAL. Take care of yourself. Don't let yourself go! If you do, he is not going to care for you sexually, regardless of how well you think you have it together.

Leave your egotistical mood swings at home

When dealing with your King, there is no time for super-inflated egos or mood swings. A busted ego has caused more downfalls to greatness than we could ever imagine. As a Virtuous Woman, your best bet is to leave your egos or mood swings at home while bringing your courage along to ensure that fear has no room to attack your Virtuous Womanship qualities. By using this principle, you are better able to help your King to get what he wants without you getting what you want first. Whether we get what we want on the front or back end will not matter if we take our ego out of the equation. And, once we understand this one principle, it will ensure that we do not have a temper tantrum when we should be mentoring and motivating our King.

Find the Problem and Solve it

We must find a way to solve a problem, whether it's our problem or our King's problem we must become a problem-solver. The way to excel in what we do, we must give people what they want, and they will give us what we want. In so many words, we must provide some sort of solution to a problem—if we desire for our Breadcrumbs of our Virtuousness to remain intact. When we make the lives of others easier, then our lives will become easier as well. A Queen such as ourselves, our attitude, our thoughts, our actions, or our reactions has no value until they are acted upon, displayed, or revealed. When we find the purpose of our Breadcrumbs or the reasons why we are sharing our Breadcrumbs, we will then be able to master our unique niche. Therefore, allowing everything to work in our favor as we avail ourselves to follow the proper order of divine protocol or code of proper behavior to be who we are, and not something or someone we are not. If you really want to see a Real Virtuous Woman at her best, just sit back and watch how she solves problems!

The Book of Esther teaches us how **NOT** to try to change our King—your goal is to understand where he's coming from, where he's at, and where he's going. This may require you to polish up those listening skills; and by doing so, you as a Virtuous Woman will enable him to experience a sense of freedom that will keep him sold out for you. My Virtuous Woman, when a man feels free with a woman, she is better able to understand him, and he will trust her to be able to understand him as well. However, you must always let him know that he has options and that you value his wants and needs; as a Virtuous Woman, this is a part of your priority in a relationship. You must consider this man's feelings regarding everything you do; as you allow him to express himself—**KEEP YOUR PAST TO A BARE MINIMUM.** You do not want to give them something to use against you; speak more about your future, not your past. As a word of caution, never expect your King to carry your baggage from previous relationships. There are some things that you may have to expose due to honest principles; but, there are some things that you are going to have to leave in the closet and vow to never expose. Everyone has a past but you never want your past to prevent you from embracing your future.

In order to establish Kingdom savvy, you and your King must discuss your likes, dislikes, fears, frustrations, and expectations of each other. This will ensure that there will not be any surprises later on in the relationship. However, it's imperative that you do not use the past to prey upon your King's insecurities. You must understand as a Virtuous Woman; he will make mistakes, and it's imperative that you do not become confrontational with your King when or if you catch him in a lie. Of course, you are his best supporter; however, you must not make excuses for his shortcomings—express your concerns without arguing, screaming, fussing or fighting. Your King is not your Child, and you never want to treat him as such.

Respectfulness is key, whether you are dealing with yourself, your King, or others. Everyone wants to be treated with respect. When we treat everyone great, the law of reciprocity will kick in to grant us greatness in that particular area of our life. When we find something good about someone or something, grace is granted to us whether we realize it or not. Believe it or not, these are the brownie points that we definitely do not want to lose. Of course, we may want to fix whatever it is or plead our case, but there are times when patience is the key. As a matter of fact, it is best not to make decisions when we are stressed, pressed or confused. Oh, by the way, this will put the icing on the cake when it comes down to us understanding the purpose behind our Virtuous

Womanship. In so many words, we are relational beings, and when we are able to relate to others effectively, it will definitely propel us in areas that most people fall short. Simply, ask God to allow the Holy Spirit to better prepare you for the adornment of your King.

Chapter 4

The Room of Power

Our turning point comes when we understand the true essence of change and universal love. Even if our lives do an about-face, we must become submissive to God, His ways, His will, and Our King, even if we don't have one yet—the willingness must be present. In order to make your turning point effective, you must understand your state of mind, as well as your state of heart regarding your potential King.

We must become very careful about the thoughts that we think about becoming a Virtuous Woman as well as attracting a King. At this very moment, there are many potential Virtuous Women who have dominating thoughts that reject quality kingdom prospects. Your life is in your hands, your thoughts are in your hands, your heart is in your hands, your Virtuous Womanship is in your hands, and your King is within your reach. If you want your Virtuous Womanship, if you want your King, and if you want your Kingdom, then it's left up to you to take the initiative to do what you need to do without becoming vindictive, defensive, emotional, or victimized.

Now, I need to know, "How bad do you want your King?" or "How bad do you want to keep your King?" When you start walking toward your King, dreaming about your King, talking about your King, praying about your King, and breathing over your King—that means you are ready; until then—you are not. Giving up too soon or not trying at all will hinder those who become stagnate in their ways of thinking when it comes down to attracting our ideal King. When we want something out of life, sitting on the couch day in and day out, is not going to get it! We must get out of our comfort zone, and do something about the situation or circumstance we are in without expecting others to do it for us. If you are waiting for someone to believe in you—stop waiting. It starts with you believing in you. As a matter of fact, no one can truly believe in you better than you can. You have what you have—work with it. You are who you are—work with it. It is what it is—work with it! If the person that you are in relations with does not fit in—it's possible that he may not be your King. Work with what you have to get the results you want; and most often, your break-through to your King is usually in your ability to stay out of the bedroom.

You cannot wish, hope, desire, and pray to meet your King and then have thoughts of not being a Virtuous Woman. What we are saying or thinking, is just as important as having what we want and desire in our Virtuous Womanship status as well. And, regardless of your status, you will have and become what you think. My Virtuous Woman, the thoughts you're planting in your mind will bring about life to its own King, so be very careful about what you are saying and thinking about you and your King. The image that you consistently hold in your mind will produce a mirror image of what you see in your mind's eye. For that reason alone, from this day forward, let your thoughts create the Virtuous Womanship or lifestyle that you truly want to manifest.

Mary, the mother of Jesus, was a very submissive woman. She understood the value of accepting the responsibility of nurturing a King, even when it did not appear so. She knew that in order for Jesus to take his rightful place in life, she must nurture him, coach him, and become devoted to God's will, and His way. Even though Jesus was her son, she did not give up on her King, and His purpose, regardless of what people said about him or how they treated Him. She was known as a Real Virtuous Woman, and she knew it was her responsibility to let her child go when she realized that he was becoming a MAN, giving him room to grow into his gift. She and her husband, realized this when they saw him teaching in the synagogue at age 12, in Luke 2:41-52. All children are not created equal, although everyone has a gift, but all gifts, talents, or callings are not the same. If a child is not a natural born basketball player, why force them to play basketball when they love soccer? If a child loves ice skating, why force them to play roller derby? If a child loves to sing, and they are forced to play the piano, it is a possibility they may rebel, in some indirect way because *"no prophet is accepted in his hometown"* Luke 4:16-30; therefore; they will find a way to break free—it's only a matter of time. *A man's gift maketh room for him, and bringeth him before great men in high places."* Proverbs 18:16.

A Virtuous Woman will not live her unfulfilled dreams through her child; she teaches her child how to build a dream on their own, and how to live it, with no excuses or regrets. She seeks out the uniqueness of her child, nurtures the uniqueness of her child, and when her child's gift is presented to the world as Jesus was presented to us. She does what Mary did—Mary Prayed for her child.

There is nothing like a Real Virtuous Praying Mother. A Real Virtuous Praying Mother can shake the roof off a house—a mother that wage spiritual warfare to protect her child carries some serious weight in the Kingdom of God. As a point of reference, the Catholics know the power of a praying mother as well. Although, I am not Catholic, I admit that everyone is entitled to their own beliefs, and I give them much respect for theirs; however, to my understanding, they use prayers to Mary the Mother of Jesus—in today's time. They have caught on to the little Breadcrumb I just dropped in your lap—the Power that Mary had in her Prayers, or the power that she may still possess? Who knows; but, can you imagine seeing your child being nailed to a cross, and all you can do is pray for him? Can you imagine your child with thorns wrapped around his head bleeding; and, all you can do is pray for him? Can you imagine someone beating your child, dragging him through the dirt weighted down with a cross on his back being humiliated, and you could not do anything, but pray for him? That's really the Power of a Praying Virtuous Mother! Now in today's time, you are not faced with that issue, and you cannot find the words to pray for your own?

We are quick to run to someone else to pray for our own, and the power is in our hands! How is that we have lost our VIRTUE? How is it that we have given our VIRTUE away? Although we are quick to fight or resort to some sort of violence; but, there is one thing I know, the power of prayer can and will move mountains! Now, that is POWER. How about the Breadcrumbs of Power that can be brought to our home by covering our children with prayers in the Name of the Father, Son, and Holy Spirit? Now, that is really the **Bread of Life**!

Chapter 5

Room of Turmoil

When we look to the left, women have a problem with me, when I look to the right; here they go again, ISSUES! Now, the true question is, "Why do people treat you the way they do?" My Virtuous Woman, people will treat you the way they see themselves, or they will treat you based on how you see YOU. So, my question is, "How do you see yourself? If you do not buy you, then what makes you think that others will buy what you are offering? That's not possible. You must find a way to believe in your Virtuous Womanship; if not, people will know or sense it, and they will treat you accordingly. People, buy YOU! Most often, we don't want to admit it, but it's the truth. If we are flaky in our image, we will become flaky in asking for people to treat us with respect. There is no reason to fast-talk, or deceive others into thinking that you are something, that you are not! Simply, learn these Virtuous Womanship principles, apply them accordingly, and watch how they provoke a change within others as you embrace the throne of your Virtuous Womanship.

When we embrace our throne as a Virtuous Woman, we must remind ourselves not to become like Lot's wife. In the Bible, we do not hear much about her; she took care of her husband and their two daughters as they traveled through the desert with Lot's uncle Abraham. Apparently, Lot's crew could not get along with Abraham's crew; so it was best that they parted ways—low and behold, Lot and his family ended up in Sodom & Gomorrah. In my opinion, it takes a Real Virtuous Woman to travel the desert with her husband, in the heat, the dust, thirsty, sweating, lack of toiletries, etc.—you get the picture......I know that's what they had to do back then; but, are there not women still doing this right now? And, we have the nerve to complain? Let me get back to the point—I had a moment.

In Genesis 19, two Angels told Lot to leave Sodom & Gomorrah, and not to look back because they were getting ready to destroy that place. They were obedient; however, Lot's wife looked back, and she became a Pillar of Salt—why did she become a pillar? In my opinion, she became crystallize out of disobedience. When God brings us into our status of Virtuous Womanship, we must not look back into our past relationships to judge our King. Our King is a unique man, and God used our past to prepare us, and not for us to use it to destroy ourselves or our King. We must not operate in disobedience; if we do, we will find that our heart will become hard. We cannot properly love our King if we allow our past to crystallize our heart, preventing us from embracing the blessings that God has for us. What's in the past should be left there, if not—it will have the potential to come back and haunt us. This is a serious matter that we take for granted, and we play on the fact that we want others to know everything about us—I must say, there are times when we need to leave well enough alone, or we will bring problems to our own house just as Lot's wife did. Although she became crystallized by looking back; but, she also destroyed her family. As a result of her disobedience, she left her two daughters to raise themselves the best way they knew how and to take care of their father. And, guess what? They picked up what they saw taking place in Sodom & Gomorrah; her two daughters got their father drunk, slept with him, and became pregnant. Yes, she was the initial cause of the abomination which is still set in motion today. Of course, we can say that we cannot blame the mother; however, I can say—yes, we can! She did not follow the instructions given to the saving of her house; and, a Real Virtuous Woman assumes total responsibility for her mistake—no one else looked back, except for her, not even to her demise! As a result, Lot is the Father of the Ammonites and the Moabites who were always fighting against their Israelite cousins. What a small world..........right?

A disobedient spirit is not worth a Virtuous Woman losing her family over, especially when it comes down to her lineage. God separated them once to put an end to the bickering, fussing, and fighting at the beginning of the story when Abraham's crew was fighting with Lot's crew. When God takes us out of something that we are emotionally or mentally attached to, we have a tendency of revisiting that place again—it is that place that robs our VIRTUE. Lot's wife was not a bad person; she was not vindictive—she was just a little emotionally caught up in a place like most women are. However, when it comes down to the saving of our house, our family, our lineage, our legacy, our family name, or our image, we must put our emotions to the side. The one moment of selfishness brought back the rivalry between Abraham's crew and Lot's crew under the generational curse that was renamed as the Ammonites & the Moabites fighting against the Israelites.

Listen to Me

Listening is one of the greatest **Breadcrumbs** known to a Virtuous Woman, and without it, she becomes limited. Furthermore, we can definitely hear more when we listen opposed to talking. People will tell you how they want to be treated, and they will also tell you why. They know what they are looking for better than anyone else, and all we have to do is "Break the ice." This can be done by asking fact-finding questions, and repeating back to them what you have heard. This will tell them that you were paying attention to them.

In the process of listening, when there is doubt about whether or not a person is your King—he is usually **NOT**! It is through our rationalizing and justification that cause us to make costly mistakes; therefore, wasting valuable time pursuing someone who's going to elude us anyway. This can be avoided if we just listen to them—listen to what they are saying, what they are not saying, listen to their body language, and listen to LIFE. Life has a way of telling you things that people are afraid to tell you; but, you must hone into LISTENING very well.

Our objective in life is to move forward and upward in our Virtuous Womanship. Upward movement is great as long as we don't allow the uppercuts of life to land us right on our face. It's imperative that we protect ourselves when moving ahead in life. When we decide to move ahead, there will always be those who are designed to get us off track. Most often, it is through our environment or conversations that we lower our guards to people, places, and things that appear to have our back. For that reason, we must evaluate our conversations carefully, because it is through the conversations that we entertain that gets us side-tracked—putting us in a position to sustain an uppercut from life that knocks us off our feet, flat on our face, or get us hit below the belt with a punch that we did not see coming. Now, in order to stay on our feet, we must understand that there are choices all around us, and it's our responsibility to choose the company that we want to keep, and the environment we want to strive in.

A person with a calm spirit will chase away a confrontational spirit; and, a confrontational person will drive away those who are adamant about keeping a calm environment. Always remember that it takes two to conversate, two to argue and one person to ruin or deflate them both. In so many words, it takes one person to say the wrong thing to ruin a conversation. However, it also takes one person to withdraw from a conversation or argument, and there will no longer be a conversation or an argument. Of course, it can and will become challenging to hold your tongue when there is turmoil. However, by doing so, it will enable you to make the right move at the right time to protect yourself, your environment, your job, your family, your friends and most of all your sanity.

As we all know, an unforgiving seed that's planted in our heart will grow into a bitter and resentful tree bearing much fruit. Many of us appearing to have it all together on the outside are afflicted with known and unknown bitterness that's eating us up from the inside. I personally know how it feels to die a slow death from the inside out in a puddle of unforgiveness and bitterness. This is a very serious problem that will destroy you, your marriage, your children, your job, your church, your Virtue, your King, and the list goes on. Beware of your actions, reactions, and body language because the fruit does not fall far from the tree, with a possibility of affecting your bloodline for generations to come. If you are harboring bitterness and resentment, it will eventually show up in some area of your life.

Our Virtuous Womanship will definitely start taking shape when we provide the mold for it. We all have the option to better ourselves or destroy ourselves by the choices we knowingly or unknowingly make on a moment-by-moment basis. I know that we make choices all the time; however, we are going to focus on the molding process that's related to our choices. As you very well know, a mold is the framework that produces an end result of what we desire. And, not only that, the molding process has a certain order, a certain pattern or a certain flow that's very distinctive in its characteristics. The only way to obtain order out of a mold is to know the end result of what we want to achieve. Once this is established, then we are better able to set specific goals regarding what **Breadcrumbs** we need to do to make our mold complete, to receive the finished product or to develop a timeline of completion.

Most often, things fall apart because we do. When we do not put things in the proper perspective, it is extremely hard for our instincts and our conscious to work hand-in-hand, which is desperately needed to ensure that things flow into its proper place. My Virtuous Woman, life is designed to accomplish a common goal, and that is to serve you. In order for life to serve you, you must know precisely what you want, how you want it, and when you want it! And, yes, God broke the mold when He created you; but, He has also set certain laws in motion to ensure that you are able to create a mold to manifest the desires of your heart. Your life is in your hands—it's time for you to use every Breadcrumb, tool, talent, or skill that you have to get what you want, positively—Never underestimate small beginnings, come out of that turmoil and go get it! You have Virtue, my Lady, share it.

Chapter 6

Jezebel's Room

When it comes down to living life, we all have something to share, but we must take into account that all Breadcrumbs are not good crumbs. There are some crumbs that must be discarded quickly, especially those that are presented to us with a Jezebel Spirit in Sheep's clothing. Most often, we think that Jezebel was a loose woman or some sort of prostitute; but, according to scripture that's not the case: According to 1 King 16, she was a Queen, the wife of King Ahab that worshiped Baal—she controlled her husband. Actually, she controlled every man in her life including her dad, King Ethbaal. In my opinion, she had no respect for her husband because she felt that he was weak for giving up his God, and having to come and serve her god. She even got her weakling of a husband to build a house for Baal so she could worship her false god. What a way to live, to go from serving God Almighty, to bowing down to a woman, serving a false god? What a blow to his manhood!

Although he was still a King in his own right, but Jezebel was calling the shots—her goal was to kill off all the prophets of God—She was the epitome of evil in sheep's clothing with the philosophy of "Taking what she wants, and will destroy any and everything that gets in her way regardless of deed, creed, or breed." She was a force to be reckoned with that negatively influenced her husband; which is the one case the God spoke openly in scripture regarding saying, *"But there was none like unto Ahab, which did sell himself to work wickedness in the sight of the Lord, whom Jezebel his wife stirred up."* 1King 21:25.

The quickest way to lose people is to control them unless that is what they like. However, we can get more out of people when we simply share information. People do not like to be told what to do—they will resist what you are presenting if you become too bossy. Bossy, Jezebel want-to-be Virtuous Women are the fast-talking women that self-destruct very quickly. The Jezebel Spirit as you now know preys on weak men or anyone that's a threat to her having her way. If it resides within you, she is very dominating, possessive, envious, defensive, arrogant, problematic, abusive, chaotic, hurts others on purpose, rude, combative, mimics others, doesn't greet people, jealous, critical, ungrateful, cruel, selfish, and manipulative; which are all negative characteristics of a fast-talker.

When you develop a positive relationship with your King, He is less likely to become remorseful of having you as his Virtuous Woman. As a matter of fact, he will become more understanding of your value and the true essence of your Virtuous Womanship when you don't try to scheme, connive, or fast-talk your way into getting what you want. Also, when you share your likes, dislikes, and concerns with your King, you actually help him to share of himself as well. Therefore, leaving little room for error or justification of whether you are a Jezebel in Sheep's Clothing. However, you must allow what happened in the past to stay in the past; rehashing issues will not produce a pretty outcome when it comes down to communicating with a King. It's imperative that you let your King know how much you need him; besides, who wants to feel unneeded? This will definitely help bring fulfillment into his life and not codependency. Your goal is to become interdependent and involved in his life, naturally. You don't have to force things to happen if it is for you—it will happen! Remember, a King will have a different genetic makeup than a Virtuous Woman. And, for that reason, he will not be driven by the same emotions that you will be—don't expect him to understand you if you are not sure you understand yourself. So, there is no need to manipulate him or anyone else.

Manipulative Anger is not characterized as a trait to possess when trying to get people to help you achieve the desires of your heart. Who doesn't become angry from time-to-time? We all will; however, anger that's used to manipulate others or to have our way as Jezebel did is another issue. When we find ourselves controlling others with our anger, we will also find that we have placed limits on our ability to communicate effectively; therefore, creating strife in our environment. Environmental strife does not solve problems; actually, it creates problems. And, until we realize what we are doing, we will continue to operate in a selfishness that creates snares of our own making. Overriding a person's will with anger is a recipe that brings about secret revenge, withdrawal, or rebellion. When we allow miscommunication to reign in our life, we will find ourselves alienated from the people who are close to us or the people we work with daily. We cannot get mad at people for not doing what we want them to do; regardless of whether he or she is our husband/wife, child, friend, employee/employer, etc. Certainly, there are times when we need to exercise tough love; but, tough love has nothing to do with manipulative anger. Now, without a doubt, we may suffer the consequences and repercussions for not doing what we need to do; however, exercising discipline out of anger is not a justifiable action. Actually, it only justifies us to think through our anger and to make a decision out of correction and not control.

Whether your anger is kept a secret or whether it is well known, it must be controlled and dealt with accordingly. This will ensure that your anger does not manifest something that will cause harm to you or deprive you of your heart's desire. It's okay to cool off before confronting a situation or circumstance that's derived out of anger. As a Virtuous Woman, your best bet is to do and say things out of humble love and not anger to prevent any form of drama in your life.

It is time out for the "Drama Virtuous Women." A true Virtuous Woman is patient; she refrains from overreacting to things she does not like. As a matter of fact, she does not expect her King to be something that he is not. She understands that she is not psychic—she does not try to read his mind because she knows that reading a person's mind leaves room for error. However, as a Virtuous Woman, she always asks fact-finding questions in the "I" form and never in the "You" form. This keeps him relaxed without her trying to figure him out or figure out the wrong thing. Choosing the way in which you communicate is key,

A Virtuous Woman "I" Form Example Fact-Finding Questions:

I am having a great time, how are you?

I am headed out to work, what on your agenda today?
I had a fabulous day today, how was your day?
I have great plans for the weekend, have you planned anything?
I have a taste for steak tonight, what do you have a taste for?

Jezebel "You" Form Example Fact-Finding Questions:

What's wrong with you? or What's your problem?
What are you doing today? or What's up today?
What did you do today? or What's up?
What are you doing for the weekend? or What's going on?
What do you feel like eating? or What's on the menu?

Shortcuts in life are not always easy or right. Sometimes when you try to make something too easy for yourself, you miss out on the most important lessons causing you to become a professional victim. Professional victims are easily frustrated and constantly driven by things that cause them to become depressed. In so many words, they subconsciously feed off the negativity in their lives. This does not make them a bad person; they just need to become more aware of what's causing them to repeat the same cycle over and over. Things may not be easy, but you can definitely make them SIMPLE. Keeping life simple will probably be the easiest way to keep your life on track without compromising or sacrificing your integrity. How do you keep life simple? Great question! Remember, there is a lesson to be learned in everything—learn the lesson, keep it positive, and move on to help and inspire others to do the same. Could it possibly be that easy? Sometimes "yes" and sometimes "no"; but this will keep you from becoming a professional victim of circumstance!

Taking our time to make wise and sound decisions will keep us on track, regardless of the type of grip that life may have on us. Thinking about what we are doing before we do it, is a great way to stay on top of our game. We have to find a way to weigh the pros and the cons before making a permanent decision regarding something or someone that's designed to be temporary

.

Chapter 7

The Sparkle

Anything that sparkles will catch our attention when it's pointed in the right direction. For a King, he loves the sparkle of an intelligent, sophisticated, and secure woman who can solve problems without being rude, nasty, or pushy. He is also attracted to a woman who does not try to make him think or act like a woman. A Real Virtuous Woman, who possesses that special spark, is not on a power-trip, she looks for little Breadcrumbs to enhance the confidence level of her Virtue to keep her spark bright.

In, 1 Samuel 25, Abigail comes to mind when it comes down to solving or helping a King to think through his decisions. Abigail was the wife of Nabal, who refused to show kindness to David and his men. She discerned that David would seek revenge on her family, so she sought him out to beg for forgiveness on her husband's behalf. Abigail brought food and gifts for David and his men. She took it upon herself to exercised Godly wisdom, and her leadership skills to solve David's dilemma to protect her family. She was absolutely correct in her discernment: David had been running from King Saul, and he had been camping out in the wilderness for some time—David needed some supplies, and I am pretty sure he and his men were starving. Nabal should have at least given the man some food—even if he could not provide David with an entourage of men to help him in battle. Especially, after being informed that it was David's men that protected his Shepherds in the Wilderness. Nevertheless, this good for nothing, stingy man sent David's men away empty handed. Abigail risked her life approaching David; however, she was not going to allow the folly of her husband to destroy her house. She was willing to take that risk, to set the record straight—she did not waste time arguing, backbiting, bad-mouthing, or fighting. This woman stepped into action. There are some times in life where a woman is called into action, where she has to just shut her mouth and handle business. I never see once in the Bible where she caused a scene or created some sort of havoc. In my opinion, life will call our virtue into action, and we must answer whether we like it or not. If she had not answered, I can only imagine what would have happened—I would say that the sparks from her Breadcrumbs shined really bright because David was so intrigued by this well-kept woman; he eventually made her his Virtuous Woman after her husband died.

It's imperative that you keep a clear mind when preparing yourself for your King; because you are your best product; and, you never know when you will be called into action. When it comes down to really attracting a King, image is very important—men subconsciously lose respect for women who do not take care of themselves. Even though they may not say anything, but they are looking, and paying attention whether you think so or not.

When we are promoting ourselves, we must keep a clear mind. We cannot focus on our problems when we are providing a solution to our King. Remember, if we listen effectively, people will tell us what they need, what they want, and how to present a solution to them. With that being said, meditate to bring your heart and mind to a place of peace before you present whatever you have to your King.

Taking Care of Your Temple

When we become too busy, we will find that we will start overlooking the basic essentials of having a balanced lifestyle. By doing so, we will also find that chaos and confusion will begin to play a dominant role. My Virtuous Woman, be very cautious about keeping yourself so busy doing stuff while forgetting about being who you are and truly living a good life. Living our lives miserably busy is a telltale sign that we need to slow down and enjoy ourselves as well as our well-being. As a matter of fact, when we are balanced in the way in which we live and take care of ourselves, we are better able to think on our feet and communicate more effectively. Regardless of what you have going on in your life, it is imperative that you take extra care to eat healthy, exercise, and get enough sleep. Don't wait for an emergency to take action. You and you alone control how you feel. Your health is essential to your well-being if you want to live long enough to enjoy your King and not to mention, your life!

Chapter 8

The Leader

Who said that a woman could not lead? There is a leader and a follower in all of us; however, it is our responsibility to know when to lead and when to follow. In Judges 4-5, we had a woman named Deborah; she was a wife, judge, prophetess, and a leader of the Israelites; but most of all, she was a fighter. She exuded great leadership skills to take the lead over her people and to be a humble, submissive wife at home. She is basically showing us how to lead, give advice, solve problems, and be a Virtuous Woman all at the same time without losing our effectiveness. She brought 40 years of peace to the Israelites; which gives us an opportunity to bring peace to our own homes. Virtuous Women are most effective when they keep peace with their King and when they keep peace in the environment. Take it from Deborah; she is a perfect example of how to lead and to allow greatness to follow in our footsteps. Nevertheless, when it was time to go to war, Deborah did not mind picking up her sword and shield and going into battle—she was God's Plan B! Or Plan A, who cares—for Barak's lack of faith, in my opinion, she handled her business! However, Deborah is designed to help us deal with the warring of a Real Virtuous Woman—yes, indeed, the hidden struggles that we all have.

Of course, assuming the role of a Virtuous Woman does not mean that you will agree with your King 100% of the time. However, it is a Virtuous Woman's responsibility to keep confusion down in her house to ensure that harmony is projected throughout her house and within her King. This can be accomplished by you, and your King working interdependently to accomplish a shared purpose or common goal. This will better enable the both of you to develop and grow spiritually, emotionally, and mentally. This does not mean that they are going to be perfect; but when there is a drive for greatness within your walls, it prevents the acts of self-sabotage. My Virtuous Woman, remember that you cannot force chemistry to work between you and your King; and if you do, it's not going to work anyway, or you will have some form of crisis.

Weakness Power

The first step to overcoming any type of weakness is to admit it! I am not saying that we have to tell everyone our business—what I am saying is that it's imperative that we admit it (the weakness) to ourselves while surrendering whatever that "IT" may be to God. Now, what I have found is that when we are weak about something or someone, we tend to deny that in which is already evident; and, when we step into a zone of denial, that means that we don't have anything to work on. In my opinion, when we tiptoe around our weaknesses, it creates a hidden desire to look for weaknesses in others to justify not dealing with our own;

therefore, creating a war from within the depths of our very own soul. An undealt with or justified weakness can become a point of entry for our enemy to break us down as a form of control or manipulation; and, if we are not careful in this aspect, an undealt with or justified weakness will also cause us to latch on to any and everything that feeds it with negative energy, or have us to second-guess an obvious strength. The war from within is what causes us to retreat from life or to embrace it, and when we look in the mirror to become honest with the true person that's looking back at us and deal with our own weaknesses, we will not have time to look for the mistakes of others. A Breadcrumb of Real Virtue is that a weakness turned inside-out, becomes a hidden strength when we channel positive energy toward it, to bring wholeness and rectification, to bless the lives of others.

Look toward Heaven from whence your strength cometh; and, rest assured that your weakness will become a hidden strength, guaranteed! For when you are weak, then you are strong. Regardless of how you may justify and rationalize your need for a King in your life, your King is designed to fill a void that only he can fill. Your King is filled with love, passion, romance, compassion, and communication; while being able to fulfill your sexual fantasies. However, if you do not have a King in your life, or if you make the wrong selection in a mate, God will not toss you to the wayside, you will have the ability to:

1. Stand on Your Own.
2. Make Decisions on Your Own.
3. Judge on Your Own.
4. Rule on Your Own.
5. Reign on Your Own.
6. Fight on Your Own.

7. Win on Your Own.

For all of the Real Virtuous Women that do not have a King as of yet. You will not be at a loss, nor will God allow you to feel that way if you trust and believe that—you do not have to settle for less. Speak only good things over your life and the lives of others. Words are designed to build up or break down the human spirit, making it very important to understand the rightful intent of what's being said. We absorb words! We all must admit that words do hurt from time-to-time. And, being that we are not made of steel, our day becomes a manifestation of our spoken words. Furthermore, most of our problems today stem from the lack of communication. When the lines of communication are broken, conflict in relationships will soon follow. Satan relies on people like you and me, to carry out the destruction of each other through profanity, mud-slinging, criticizing, complaining, and judging. Just as we can encourage someone without knowing it, we can just as well discourage someone without knowing it as well.

Words taken out of context, or perceived out of context can inadvertently leave a bad taste in someone's mouth. For that reason, it is very important that we keep the lines of communication open because the way we start a conversation will determine how it will end. Choose your words carefully to ensure that you do not unintentionally inflict wounds that may or may not heal. Simply, remain positive, NO MATTER WHAT! Just remember, there is life and death in the power of the tongue, so speak LIFE into the lives of others and into your life as well. This is a sure way of always finding the right words to say at the right time.

Chapter 9

The Anointing

We must understand that people really build, or tear down our credibility with or without our consent. Of course, there are certain mysteries about our life that we may not be able to decipher; however, we are able to learn from others to ensure that we are not making the same mistakes. And, that mistake is with those who really are Virtuous by Design—that means that they are anointed with a certain type of Virtue. When a person has a Breadcrumb Anointing, they are really gifted by God in a certain area to reach certain people for a God-given purpose. They have a set path, and God will rain fire and brimstone to keep them on that certain path as he did for Moses in the Book of Exodus.

We often forget about some of the qualities of Miriam, the sister of Moses. According to Exodus 2, she was the one who watched her brother float down the river to protect him from being killed. It was through Miriam's ability to think on her feet that kept her brother alive. She also stood by her brother's side through all the trials; even though, she spoke against him out of jealousy at one time. Being that Miriam knew her little brother's strengths and weaknesses—she became frustrated with his decision-making process, and his ability to be an anointed leader with faults. Therefore, out of her anger, she questioned his ability to hear the Voice of God. Soon thereafter, she was struck with leprosy, and placed outside of the camp. However, she repented, asked for God's forgiveness, and got back into her rightful place of supporting her brother physically, mentally, and emotionally; as well as a prophetess to his needs, and the needs of the Children of Israel. Her story lets us know that we will make mistakes; but, we must quickly repent ensuring that we are able to properly support our King. We need to be able to think on our feet to ensure that we are able to protect our King even if we don't agree with the purpose of God in his life.

We must become very cautious to contain our jealousy; even if we walk in our own Gifting or Calling—do not knock your King or the Calling of someone who is in his or her rightful place. People will be who they are, whether we want them to or not. When we share our love, compassion, and generosity, people tell others, and if it's negative, people will tell that as well. People have influence over others, and they tell people what they have experienced, or how they have positively or negatively felt. This is a reality, and if they like you—they will tell at least 9 other people about you. However, this cycle can and will work both positively and negatively; so we must find a way to keep it on the positive end of the scale to produce the results that we truly desire. And, what is our end result? It is to attract and keep your King by finding that hidden coin or missing coin from within. In Luke 15:8-10, Jesus paints the ideal picture, *"Or suppose a woman has ten silver coins and loses one. Doesn't she light a lamp, sweep the house and search carefully until she finds it? And when she finds it, she calls her friends and neighbors together and says, 'Rejoice with me; I have found my lost coin.' In the same way, I tell you, there is rejoicing in the presence of the angels of God over one sinner who repents."*

The factor of appreciation has the power to take us a lot further than buying our way through life. How often do we show appreciation to the people, places, and things around us? If we really take a look within ourselves, we will find that we sometimes forget to say "Thank-you" or "I appreciate you" quite often. Furthermore, the lack of appreciation will cause the best of us to feel like a victim or feel as if we are being used; therefore, causing our natural defense system to kick into high gear. Of course, our ego contributes to some form of selfishness; however, it does not supersede the power of a simple "Thank-you" or "I appreciate you." Saying it is just as important as showing it; regardless of whether we feel as if it is deserved or not. Appreciation is not bought; it is given—buying our way through life will only get us so far. As a matter of fact, we will never see appreciation packaged on a shelf; however, we are able to give something as a token of our appreciation, but when it comes down to true appreciation— we cannot put a price tag on it. Let nothing take the place of a simple "Thank-you" or "I appreciate you." And, if you want to be appreciated, simply give appreciation with no strings attached.

My Virtuous Woman, I am going to let you in on a little secret—giving God thanks for the little simple things has much more substance than only thanking Him for the big things in life. So, in all things give thanks.

Know What You Are Working With
Before a King chooses you, he will want to know what you have to offer and how it's going to benefit him. My Virtuous Woman,

you must know your product; meaning—you must know YOU from the inside out! And, having a weak backbone does not always mean that you are a weak person—it just means that you will fall quickly. Regardless of whether we find ourselves falling for the okey-doke, falling by the wayside, falling mentally/emotionally, falling on our face, or falling in our faith, it is a fall indeed. A weak backbone creates a sense of desperation: desperate for love, desperate for a friend, desperate to be seen, desperate for control, desperate for attention, desperate to be at the top, desperate, desperate, desperate, and the list goes on. A desperate spirit does not attract quality people; it attracts those who feed off of desperate people. BEWARE!!!! There is nothing wrong with humbling yourself with a little prayer. Humility is the true sign of controllable strength. As a matter of fact, humility is the main ingredient that prevents you from becoming snobbish, rude, arrogant, selfish, inconsiderate, or disrespectful.

My Virtuous Woman, this is your opportunity to make the turn-around to embrace true greatness while others talk, yearn, and waste time. This will help you present the benefits without sounding scripted or fake, even though a King will buy into things day in and day out; but, when it comes down to his Virtuous Woman, he does not like to be sold—He likes being coached. In order to coach our King effectively, we must know the what, when, where, how, and why's of what we are offering him. Furthermore, a King will become sold-out to a Virtuous Woman that he wants, more-so than a Virtuous Woman that he needs. So, as a Virtuous Woman, you must find a way to cater to the want, and coach the need, to ensure all of our bases are covered, while providing an advantage or a feeling worth remembering. Don't forget to empathize and identify with the wants and needs while exercising patience with him.

A Virtuous Woman knows that timing is everything and without time, we have nothing! The face value of patience resides within us all until we allow impatience to rule over us. Furthermore, patience keeps our spirit calm, while impatience is designed to keep our spirit disrupted, anxious, and intolerant. Patience is designed to keep our emotions under control and the minute we become impatient, it causes our emotions to become out of control. As a matter of fact, a secretly impatient person is often found out through their inability to control their emotions.

Of course, we are all emotional beings, and it is our responsibility to set the tone for what, whom, why, and how we reveal our emotions. And, if we don't set the tone, then our emotions will do it for us! Our emotions have been and still are one of the biggest contributors to the downfall of men and women alike. If we don't want to become a statistic, then we must find a way to control our emotions to better control our life and our destiny. The code of patience is to be careful about making decisions when you are emotional and to be careful about becoming emotional when making decisions. This will definitely keep your mind clear about what you are thinking, doing, or becoming involved in. When you break this code of patience, you will find that bad decisions are made, when they could have been avoided.

Chapter 10

Threshing Room

In the Book of Ruth, there is a great story of Virtue that teaches us about unwavering faithfulness. You will find that Ruth had a lot of tragedy in her life as we all have at some point. However, Ruth had a way of serving people as a vessel of love, despite her hardships, and lack.

After Ruth lost her husband, she still clung to her mother-in-law, Naomi; they both decided to move in faith, back to Judah. Ruth's sister-in-law, Orpah, decided to go her own way, leaving Ruth and Naomi to take care of themselves. There are certain times when people will walk away from us, and there are times when people will stay with us; but, usually when we find ourselves going through something, we will find ourselves alone. However, Ruth did not have the heart to leave Naomi alone after her husband, and both of her sons died. Yes, bad things do happen to good people, but it does not mean that we should abandon them or neglect him or her because of their time of difficulty.

During our Virtuous Threshing, we will be tested in this manner. It will be left up to us whether or not we can become a committed person regardless of the circumstance, or event that's presented to us. Ruth's thoughts, actions, and reactions were indications of Godly character that could be used in attracting her King. My Virtuous Woman, we will not attract Kingdom Material if we give up on people easily. Rest assured, when our King is presented to us; most often, he will not appear to be that in which is designed to bless us, and for us to be a blessing to.

When Ruth went back to Judah, God granted her divine wisdom and favor by her actions. Ruth knew that out of her commitment to do good that God was going to bless her because she did not mind sharing with others. As a result, Ruth went into the field to gather up the grain leftovers to ensure that she and Naomi were able to eat. She would do this every day, and with each day, more grain was left behind as Boaz took an interest in her. As time went on, Naomi knew that Boaz was taking an interest in Ruth, so she coached her on what to do at the appropriate time—she basically taught Ruth some basic principles on how to snag her KING.

When snagging your king, you must have a good understanding of the Threshing Floor. This is basically, your sifting process, where sorting your oats takes place. When I speak of sorting your oats—you must sift the good and the bad, the right and the wrong, etc. In so many words, you must sift the negative from the positive to become totally refined or redefined for yourself, and your King. Of course, we often overlook our sifting process, our breadcrumbs, or pick up the left-overs, because no one wants to correct that in which they are comfortable with.

How can we have less and think that it's more? It's all in the matter of the heart—if we think of ourselves more than we ought, we will find that we will want more and more without becoming grateful for what we have. Most often, we associate success with things like money, power, and sex; however, less becomes more when we become naturally driven to achieve outside of the power, money, and sex. The question still remains, "If we don't have power what would we do, If we don't have money, what would we do, or If we don't have sex, what would we do?" These are valid questions that we must honestly answer to enable our less to become more. Although, we do need money to take care of ourselves and our family, we do need power to train up a child in the way that they shall go, and we do need sex to be fruitful and multiply, but they need to be put in their proper perspective. The LOVE of these 3 things can and will be the root cause of our demise. If we take a moment to look around us, most relationships, marriages, friendships, and jobs crumble because of these 3 things that we desire. It doesn't matter where we are in life from the pulpit, strip joint, to the want-to-be virtuous woman—this is applicable to all who have not put people, places, and things in their proper perspective. In my opinion, if we are grateful for less, God will bless us with more naturally; however, if we become caught up in material means, we will wind up with less—in so many words, we will find ourselves losing more than we gain. Ruth is a prime example how humility can become our best asset.

Your trials and tribulations will come as a testament to your faith. As a matter of fact, it took Naomi to point out a few things that Ruth may have overlooked. Even though Naomi was playing matchmaker, she knew what it was going to take to snag a man with Kingdom Credentials and she also knew that Ruth was teachable.

My Virtuous Woman, if you want the riffraff, you might as well turn in your crown; remember, like attracts like and this is what the Threshing Floor is all about—Be ye different. You must separate yourself from people, places, and things that are going in the opposite direction of what you desire. And, with that being said, you must protect the purity that you have from within by submitting yourself to the will of your King; if not, you will find that you will begin to choke on life. When you have too many agendas going on at the same time, conflict is inevitable.

When you are at the Threshing Floor or when you are presented with the right opportunity you must:

1. **Wash Yourself.** Take care of your personal hygiene. A Virtuous Woman will make sure that she grooms herself properly before approaching her King. Esther groomed herself for a year before she approached her King.

2. **Anoint Yourself.** Put on your make-up, do your hair, etc. while anointing yourself in the Holy Spirit.

3. **Put on Your Best Garment.** Put on an outfit that is of good taste. A Virtuous Woman's appearance is very important.

4. **Take Your Place.** Position yourself to meet your King. This is where getting fact-finding information comes into play.

5. **Respect His Space.** Do not intrude upon his social time. Wait for your time to ensure that you do not become too needy. A King will run from needy women, and if he does not he should!

6. **Do Not Pursue Him.**
7. **Make Yourself Known At The Appropriate Time.**
8. **Lie Down At His Feet.** (Kindness that others are not willing to show, cuddly.) For example, when a dog needs attention or wants your friendship—you will find that a dog will lie at your feet. Putting things at his feet is a definite sign of Humility, Trust, and Commitment. My Virtuous Woman, we often look at feet as something demeaning; however, it is in the power of our feet that our strength rest.

The best way to find out the character of a person is to watch how they treat others. When we find a person who is constantly fighting with others or instigating conflict, they are usually in a serious battle with themselves. As a matter of fact, a nagging person usually nags at himself or herself first and then takes it out on others. When we encounter a person who constantly causes or who are always involved in conflict, BEWARE! Basically, conflict is really the silent motivator of change for those who desire it; however, it can also become the downfall to those who choose to ignore it. When we find the source of our conflict, we will then find the solution. Think about it, whether we admit it or not, it is through our conflicting struggles that spark the desire for change. God will not allow conflicting free-loaders to trample over you as long as you make it your business not to trample on others. There is a purpose for everything that you go through; however, you must not lose your faith. Regardless of how it may seem, whether you are on your last, and against all odds, do good to others and your blessings will come through people, places, and things you least expect. Just know that conflict may come but it is up to you to deflate the conflict to prevent yourself from becoming too emotional. My Virtuous Woman, have fun, enjoy life and enjoy the journey while kindly thinking positive and happy thoughts.

As a result, she got her King as he considered her a woman of excellence. And, not only did she get her King, she received a blessed lineage that eventually brought about Jesus Christ, our Lord and Savior; with that being said, the lineage of your Kings is determined by your actions, reactions, attitude, and character. So, do good to ensure that your lineage will remain blessed. Be thankful for where you are, where you are not, where you are going, what's to come, and anything in between—Be Thankful.

Chapter 11

The Cord

When we have to protect our King, I often think about Rahab in Joshua 2. We often think of Rahab as being a prostitute; however, she stood behind the mission of God as she risked her own life to hide spies in her home. She also knew that she would perish if she did not act on God's behalf. However, let me break it down for you, Rahab may have been a prostitute by occupation, but she was definitely not a prostitute by **Virtue**. Just remember, that God will use anything and anyone who will accomplish His mission in total faith. Yes, she did have a struggle of being a prostitute; but regardless of the way she made her living, her faith superseded the life in which she was living. Out of her act of obedience, willingness to help, and peace, her life was spared; as a result, she was also in the lineage of Jesus Christ as well—so that should tell us something. No matter where you are in life today, you are a Virtuous Woman, who has a Virtuous Womanship waiting on you.

As we get back to the life of this bad girl Rahab, she was bad alright—she knew how to handle her business, and she knew how to keep the Men of God safe. To me, that says that she pays attention—she was not the type of woman that was careless. In my opinion, she was indeed faithful, and she had enough sense to get a promise from the spies that would spare her family. As a symbol of their agreement, there was a scarlet cord placed in the window—I would consider that a smart woman, regardless of her occupation—she did not get caught up without a plan!

When we have or desire to have a King in our life we must act in faith, and stay away from one-sided conversations, people who make you feel bad about your past or people who make you feel bad about who you are, or what you do. They have a way of only giving us half of the story. My Virtuous Woman, the Breadcrumb cord that Rehab leaves behind is that there will always be 3 sides to every story—your side, the other person's side, and the truth. When making decisions, we must evaluate all three; if not, we will find ourselves making permanent decisions on one-sided information. **Rehab's 3-Sided philosophy**: **Their side:** The spies needed help spying out the land (their goal was to take over the land); **Her side**: She wanted to save her family; **The Truth**: This Land was promised to the Children of Israel, and with or without her help—they were taking the land.

It is imperative to look at things from a different perspective. This will definitely help us in the decision-making process to ensure that we are making the best, and the wisest decisions based on the information that we have in front of us. Now with that being said, why do we often hold on to people, places, and things that are not working or entertaining people, places, and things that are counterproductive? We can say that it's fear, we can say that it's guilt, we can say that it's out of obligation, we can say that it's a lot of things; but, the truth is that most often we settle because we don't want to ask questions, or we only get half of the story. Now, in order to get the proper feedback, we must ask open-ended questions, eliminating the "yes" or "no" answers.

Making decisions without having the facts presented to us will eventually cause us to make unnecessary mistakes. Yes, we are able to learn from our mistakes; however, some mistakes can be avoided by taking a moment to think through, and ask questions about our decision-making process. My Virtuous Woman, it's good to ask questions. It's okay to know the details when it comes down to you and your well-being. Always remember, most bad decisions are derived out of impatience or the lack of information. From now on, take a little more time to get the facts to ensure that you have good, sound, and quality information when dealing with your king!

As life would have it is amazing how everyone wants to give a person a label just like they gave Rahab a label; but, let me finish the storyline for you—Rahab decides to change her life to become a Real Virtuous Woman. She marries one of the spies named Salmon. She and Salmon gave birth to a son named Boaz, Boaz married Ruth, and they gave birth to a son named Obed; Obed is the father of Jessie, and Jessie is the Father of King David, and that qualifies Rahab as a Great-Great-Grand Mother of a King! It's amazing how a label can give you so much **VALOR** and **VIRTUE** when God is on your side!

Chapter 12

Overcoming The Trickster

God looks at the heart of a Virtuous Woman. A true Virtuous Woman is caring like Rebekah when she drew the water for the camels as well as the servants of Abraham. She was a gorgeous, hard-working woman who did not mind serving those who are in need. We as Virtuous Women, miss out on the fact that we are designed to serve out of the kindness of our heart. All too often, we miss out on our Kings, because we lack the ability to recognize a need before it's actually verbalized. This is indeed what opened the door to Rebekah's Virtuous Womanship and her legacy. Although, she is not without fault; she recognized the need to serve with the ability to lead as she became the wife of Isaac, the son of Abraham. This is the secret of Rebekah and how she snagged her King, and the rest is history.

After finally conceiving, she was having a tough time during her pregnancy; and after she finally got fed up with the struggle from within, she prayed to God about it. He informed her that she was pregnant with two Nations according to Genesis 25, and the Older would serve the Younger. These two boys were fighting in the womb, fighting coming out of the womb, fighting as children, fighting as teens, fighting as adults, fighting for status, fighting for birthrights; as a matter of fact, they fought for everything since the moment they were conceived—I would consider this was sibling rivalry at its best.

The most amazing thing about Rebekah is that once she became the wife of Isaac, she somehow lost her Virtue. How often once a Virtuous Woman gets what she wants, then she switches out? She did not communicate with her husband effectively. Or, did he stop communicating with her because she constantly fought with him? Better yet, did she mark her children by constantly arguing and nagging? As scripture would have it, it took her over 20 years for her to conceive, and 20 years of nagging and arguing about her barrenness would drive any man insane! As a point of reference, children will mimic what they are taught—they had to learn how to fight each other from somewhere. Children are impressionable, and they will begin to practice what they see.

After the birth of Esau and Jacob—there was blatant favoritism between the siblings—it seems as if Rebekah was obsessed with the promise of her eldest son serving the youngest son, not realizing it was not her responsibility to make it happen. She did not tell Isaac about what God told her; she kept the secret to herself, and tried to force God's hand. If God gives us a promise, we do not need to make arrangements for Him; He is God all by himself—He does not need our help. It took years for God to unravel the mess that Rebekah got Jacob entangled in.

As Rebekah continued on her mission to play god, she divided her house with her own hands, she turned Jacob (God's Leading Man) into a houseboy, she taught him how to cook and hang around the camp all day—how in the world is he going to lead a nation hanging around the tents under the umbrella of a trickster? The once Virtuous Woman turned trickster, eavesdrops, plots, deceives her husband, plays on his vulnerability of blindness, and then she puts her favorite son, Jacob up to deceive his own father, to pretend like he is his brother to **steal** the blessing. What type of woman is this? Could she not see her family falling apart? Of course, she did—she did not care because she said, *"My son, let the curse fall on me. Just do what I say;"* Gen 27:13. After Jacob had stolen the blessing, she sent him packing to her brother Laban's house, so that his brother Esau would not kill him. What a plan! She was willing to lose her child—never seeing him again for a stolen blessing; what kind of mother is this? After that stolen blessing, we don't hear much about her in the Bible (it seems as if she was blotted out)—what a way to lose your favorite son. But, make no mistake about it, there was a great price to pay for that lost virtue, her deception, her trickster mentality, the betrayal of her husband (God's Chosen One), and those stolen blessings. Although she was responsible for her role in this matter; however, Jacob, was a grown man; and, God held him accountable for his actions as well.

Do you really think that God was going to bless that type of behavior? Do you really think that God was going to place Jacob in charge of a nation without correcting his trickster mentality? Before God made a great nation out of Jacob, he had to suffer. God had to drive that waywardness out of him, to ensure that he would be able to lead His people. Due to Jacob's behavior, fighting with his brother, betraying his brother and father, his waywardness with his trickster mentality that he learned from his mother, and outright stealing. He was forced on a journey to drive those negative Breadcrumbs out of him. The blessing that

God has for you has your name on it. You do not have to steal it. You do not have to manipulate anyone to get it. You do not have to force someone's hand in it. What is yours will be. Guaranteed!

Chapter 13
Living Water

We as Virtuous Women are not designed to be a Virtuous Woman without a voice. We are designed to speak up for ourselves while encouraging others in the things of the Lord. According to John 4, the Samaritan Woman who met Jesus at the well was a little insecure about her lifestyle of having several husbands. Jesus ministered to her needs by asking for a drink of water to test her heart; even though she did not realize what he was doing—she resisted out of custom, due to the prejudice and conflict that was common among the Samaritans and Jews. However, Jesus minister to her needs of "Living Water" to quench a thirst that resided within her; she instantly became a mouthpiece to minister to the needs of her townsmen. Not only that, she took the initiative to learn how to minister to her husband to ensure that she would not thirst again for another man.

When you understand the value of ministering to the needs of your King, you will find that he will not run from woman to woman to get what you have to give; and, you will not have to run from man to man to get what he has to give. There is "Living Water" in a Virtuous Woman, and once you share this water with others, it will quench a thirst or longing for what we do not have. However, you cannot become prejudice or selfish with the "Living Water" that's inside of you. You are designed to minister and encourage others; especially, your King.

In ministering living water, you must think good thoughts about yourself, and saturate your mind with the Word of God and good positive thoughts. The true essence of our strength lies in our ability to use our mind to better govern our attitude, actions, and reactions. The thoughts that we think, the actions that we take and our reactions create a magnetic force that pulls likeness into our personal space when we least expect it. We are the culprits to what we allow in our personal space, and the positive or negative force that surrounds us as did the Samaritan Woman. Of course, this is not done intentionally. In fact, most of the time, we don't even realize what's actually causing the positive and negative things to flow in and out of our lives.

The Samaritan Woman became a magnet after her 1st cup of living water from Jesus. Magnets attract things that fit into its magnetic field; while repelling any and all things that do not fit. Actually, we may not always draw the very same thing to us; we may simply draw someone or something of a similar kind to us. Meaning that the quality may be different, but it contains some of the same ingredients or characteristics that will still create a positive or negative bonding process. Actually, this is why two people who appear opposite are attracted to each other.

Just remember that we are all unique in our own way, but we do have similar qualities like a fingerprint. For example, everyone has a fingerprint with similar qualities, but yet different in a small minute way setting us apart from anyone else. My Virtuous

Woman, that small minute part for us, is the way we think, act, or react to our living water! Yes, the way we think, act, or react can and will positively or negatively set us apart like oil and water. Now that you understand the power of a magnet, you should never get upset when something attaches itself to you or detaches itself from you. Your best bet is to stop worrying about people, places, and things that don't click with you. If someone or something moves outside, abuse, or misuse the boundaries that you have set for yourself—you must then check or question whether they are designed to be there anyway. Oh, by the way, the best thing about a magnet is that it's not glued to you, you can just pull it apart, or withdraw at any time you feel the need to do so.

The Power of the Well

Every time we open our mouth, we are the well. If we are thirsty, it is known, without us having to say one word. If we are not thirsty, it is known. As a Virtuous Woman, the power of our well does not reside in judging another woman just because of her 5 husbands. The Samaritan Woman was looked down on because of her promiscuity or better yet, her multiple relationships so to speak. She tried to hide her relationships from Jesus, due to the fact that she was constantly being judged because her relationships were not working out.

The moral of the story is that even if you are an outcast, you have been around the block a few times, or have a bad reputation with men—all hope is not lost. Life has a way of blindsiding us with the things that we neglect dealing with; while hitting us below the belt. The neglect or the refusal to prepare leaves an open door for excuses that will eventually hinder our progress whether we like it or not. If you want more, you are definitely going to have to prepare for more of what you do have and what you don't have as well. Preparation is the key to excelling beyond the limits of your own making.

When we stop learning, whatever we are doing starts to decrease. Our best bet, is not to become defensive when others are sharing information with us or when we need to pick up a book to brush up or polish up our skills. The moment we stop learning, we start to become hard-headed and our ego will have to start filling in the gaps with inconsistency.

Consistency is the ability to follow-through when we are tempted to brush the 'need to do' under the rug. How often are we tempted to sweep things under the rug in order to not deal with them? It is all too often, of course. The best part of our follow-through is being able to consistently follow-up on ourselves. God will meet us at the point of our need—all we need to do is become consistent with being able to follow-up on the people, places, and things in our lives. And, brushing things under the rug is not the most beneficial way to get rid of anything—it will only cause things to pile up, causing us to attract parasitic relationships that suck the life out of us. How do you determine who or what's parasitic? They are usually the people, places, and things that make you feel bad about your past, or make you feel bad about being who you are. However, it's not limited to feelings; it could also be the people, places, and things that hinder your developmental process. And, for that reason, we must follow-up with ourselves, our spouse, our children, our extended family, our friends, our clients, and most of all, we must follow-up with God.

My Virtuous Woman, you need the people who are positive and supportive of who you are and not those who are negative or demeaning. Today is your day to get rid of the excess parasitic dirt that's hanging out in your life to threaten your developmental process to ensure that you are able to "Do You."

The well of unconditional love is open to you if you are willing to receive it with an open heart. Things will not always go the way you have planned; but, you can never lose your Virtue just because people become insensitive to your situation. If you feel the need to put your sexual past, or partners behind you, do it—if not, that is your prerogative. Keep your head up high, pray about it, assume responsibility for your role in the situation, share your Breadcrumb from the lesson you have learned from the situation, and be happy. That is the true Power of the Well—you are it, and it can't get any better than that!

Chapter 14

Private Room Issue

The Bible speaks of the woman with the issue of blood was healed by her ability to reach beyond her self-imposed limitations to grab the hem of Jesus' garment. According to people, they wanted her to die with this issue; however, her faith would not allow her to do so. Although she was an outcast, she did not care; she had battled with this sickness for 12 long years; and, she was not going to go through that much turmoil to only give up on herself. When a woman has an issue that will not go away, she must leave no stone unturned—that meant, she had to push her way through the crowd; she had to do something. Can you imagine having this issue for 1 year, 5 years, and how about 12 years straight? One can only imagine what she was going through—if she would have listened to all of the nay-sayers; she would not have received her healing. But, let me take a moment to break it down for you why this woman laid her faith on the line for her healing—the woman was considered unclean. Therefore, she was treated like she had a plague—nobody, including her husband, would not touch her, eat from her, sit behind her, or touch anything that she has touched. The bottom line is that this woman was isolated and lonely for 12 years! To add insult to injury, she spent all of her money trying to get better, but to no avail. I guess, when all you have left is your faith, you learn how to use it! What a life, in my opinion, she had to be some sort of depressed being treated like a leper.

This story is designed to provide healing to all of our Virtuous Women today. This woman opened the door to our ability to reach beyond our issues to embrace our King. All we need to do is pay attention and avail ourselves to reach out at the appropriate time. My Virtuous Woman, your healing is inside of you, and due to the issues that have plagued you for years—now is your time to embrace the King that rightly belongs to you. Of course, it's going to take a little patience on your part; however, when the time is right—don't be ashamed to reach out to him.

Your King needs what you have to offer, so don't allow your issues to prevent you from healing. My Virtuous Woman, you are your best asset, and you can also become your best liability; so, keep your business to yourself, and when your King comes—just touch the hem of his garment, even if your balance is off.

Our equilibrium is developed when we free our minds to do the difficult things that stifle our creativity. Entertaining the thought of something being hard is much more difficult than just freeing our mind to do the task at hand. A divided mind puts a damper on our creativity, keeping us from focusing while at the same time creating an imbalance in our life. My Virtuous Woman, there is no need to waste our time toying around with people, places, and things when our balance is off. Our off-centeredness is a breeding ground for us to become easy prey, or better yet, WEAK. As a matter of fact, it is through our weakness in life that we close our mind to our own creativity causing us to live our lives through other people. Our load, our issues, and our weaknesses become much lighter when we are able to focus and reach out to our King.

Our inability to focus will weigh us down much more than simply freeing our mind to do what we need to do in life. Counterproductive thoughts have a way of inhibiting your ability to get things done or be in the right place at the right time. My Virtuous Woman, when or if you find yourself pondering over something being difficult, you can use that same amount of time getting the task accomplished. And, yes, you are blessed with the tools needed to get the job done, but you must do the legwork without fearing the superficial façade of things being too hard. Reach out; your King is waiting for you to draw the line in the sand.

Chapter 15

Drawing The Line

Our Virtuous Womanship abilities are wrapped in our ability to draw a line in the sand on our past. We as Virtuous Women cannot allow what we have done in the past to prevent us from inheriting the throne. People may chase you around and try to stone you like they did the Adulterous Woman. However, we must walk away just as she did to seek forgiveness. Even though she was caught in the act, people were judging her without taking into account their own shortcomings in life.

Drawing a line in the sand is required to get rid of excess baggage that continues to weigh us down, jeopardizing our future of greatness. When Jesus drew a line in the sand, it separated the adulterous woman from her past giving her an opportunity to repent and change. Regardless of how people may look at you for wanting to be a Virtuous Woman, you must know that Jesus has already put a line between you and your past. My Virtuous Woman, get up and walk away from the temptations that will detour you from embracing your King or embarrassing your King.

Life changing choices will cause the best of us to revamp our perspectives in order to get things back on track. What do you do when your life jumps the track? It's real simple, get it back on track. Now, the challenge is, knowing how to get your life back on track. My Virtuous Woman, the first step to getting back on track is to know "how" and "why" you got off track in the first place. The lack of understanding can and will cause us to challenge that in which we have not taken the time to learn. My Virtuous Woman, regardless of where we are in life or what we may have accomplished, we will always have choices, problems, and decisions. Once we understand our choices, problems, and decisions, we are better able to find a solution for all three to keep balance and harmony in our lives. As a Virtuous Woman, it's okay when you have to revamp some things in your life—it keeps you open to change. In my opinion, anything that's worth having requires you to be flexible, to move when necessary and focused enough to revamp the things that most people overlook. When you find a purpose for your potential, you are better able to govern the change or the redirection of the energy pertaining to it. So, make sure that the track you are on is the right one, keeping the line drawn in the sand—separating your past from your future to protect your Virtuous Womanship inheritance, regardless of who's casting stones at you.

Stones can come from the North, South, East, and West, but the greatest encourager known to man is the encourager that resides within oneself. We are our best cheerleader, and we can also become our worst critic. Whichever one we choose, our life will become a direct reflection of that particular choice. There are times when we become so caught up in the busyness of life that we don't take the time to encourage ourselves. Therefore, we look for and expect others to do what we have not taken the time to do. My Virtuous Woman, we cannot expect others to do that in which we are not willing to do for ourselves; regardless of whether we are the encourager or the encouragee, we all need some form of encouragement.

You are the one who possess the tightest grip on your future—will you drop the ball, or will you run your own race? My Virtuous Woman, regardless of where you are in life, you can encourage yourself. You can be the best you—you can be whatever you desire, as long as you do not give up on your greatest supporter, and that is YOU. And, don't forget, after you encourage yourself, make sure you encourage someone else to activate the law of reciprocity.

Who Cares—Do you!

A Virtuous Woman will learn how to do her own thing. She may or may not include her King, depending on her lifestyle or activity. However, she has her own life outside of her Kingdom responsibilities. My Virtuous Woman, it's okay and acceptable to have your own thing going on outside of your King.

As a Virtuous Woman, our strength can easily be found when we have our emotions and mind under control with an irrevocable desire to succeed. As a matter of fact, with or without our permission, our emotions will be tested to determine our Virtuous Womanship qualities. And, it is through the testing phase that will determine our level of courage. Most often, we get so caught up in doing things to exemplify our strength in a particular area, when a Virtuous Woman's real strength comes from within.

As a Virtuous Woman, we are required to take action when accomplishing a task or goal; however, if we are distraught, confused, emotional, or miserable doing it—then what do we have? We have instability and not strength. Of course, we will all have our burdens to bear, and having our emotions under control will help us to manage our thoughts and feelings to ensure that we have enough strength to get up when we fall short. The feeling of disempowerment has a viable way of causing us to become resistant to change or to become resistant to responsibility. Furthermore, our greatest strength will not always be found in our ability to be strong; it may be in our ability to ask for help, our ability to become humble, our availability to be a helper, or our ability to be the true person that we are. You are free to think and feel however you want. Yet and still, the more you positively exercise your mind and guard your emotions, the more strength you will have in your walk of Faith. However, the key is that you must not allow it to take precedence over your King, or to cause you to appear needy.

The neediness of those who refuse to help themselves will fall prey to the victim mentality; unless, they strive a little harder to stand up on their own two feet. The best thing that we can ever do for ourselves is to stand up on our own two feet. When we become too needy, we will find that people will start to pull away from us to seek their own space. And, for that reason, we must become mindful of our wants, and needs to ensure that we are not placing any false expectations on people, places, and things that are not obligated to fulfill our needs anyway.

My Virtuous Woman, you must value doing you, simply because if you don't know, you will find yourself becoming clingy. Men do not like clingy women! Clinginess is an automatic sign of insecurity—you must give your King some room to breathe. Yes, you are a Virtuous Woman, and a Virtuous Woman is not designed to cling to people, places, and things. She is designed to embrace people, places, and things with her essence of balance— she cannot overdo, or overstay her welcome. In so many words, a

Virtuous Woman cannot sit around and lollygag at her friend's house all day when she has things to do, places to go, and other people to see.

Chapter 16

Breadcrumbs of a Woman

When we talk about a Breadcrumb, the average woman will look down on a Breadcrumb because she would not realize its value. In my opinion, she would not see its value due to the fact that it is not designed for her to see unless she voluntarily takes her blinders off. The value is not necessarily in the physical Breadcrumb—the value lies in the Spirit. This is indeed of the Spirit—it is a Spiritual Breadcrumb, and it is designed for a woman to turn her nose up when she is not ready for it. As life would have it, once she lives a little longer; and life turns her upside down—soon turning her sexy curves into lumpy bumps; she will eventually come searching for that Breadcrumb. Actually, she will come searching for that anything to make that hidden pain go away. These are the Breadcrumbs that are overlooked the most, yet are the most POWERFUL. Our Breadcrumbs may come as a lesson, principles, character traits, instincts, the eloquence, a matter of integrity, a forewarning that justice is in full armor, or an impartation of wisdom. However, our

Breadcrumbs are not limited, nor can we limit them; and, that is why we must keep our element of Virtue in full effect at all times. Our Breadcrumbs are here to feed us on a moment-by-moment basis through the power of the HOLY SPIRIT, and it is only He that knows what we need before we do. The Proverbs 31 Woman knew the value of connecting to her Breadcrumbs, and so should you.

Of course, we all know something about the Proverbs 31 Woman; but do we really know the Breadcrumbs of the ideal Proverbs 31 Woman? According to Proverbs 31, this woman kept her home, she ran her own business, she was a seamstress, took care of her garden, she shopped, and taught her family wisdom, and most of all, she was grateful.

When we place value in the true essence of our gratefulness, we will then open ourselves up to the invincible Breadcrumbs of wisdom. The hidden Breadcrumbs of wisdom are wrapped up in everyday living. The Proverbs 31 Woman knew that every day was designed to teach her something, she also knew that every day was designed to give her something, and she knew that every day was designed to take something away. Regardless, of how she saw life, she knew that life was doing what it was designed to do. So, she prepared herself daily. And, sometimes, life has a way of asking us, "What are we doing with our life?" Or, it may ask us, "Are we doing what we are designed to do?" When we become grateful where we are, we will better understand where we are going. It is our awareness of truth, which provokes the inner wisdom from within as it did for the Proverbs 31 Woman. As a matter of fact, when we lie and deceive ourselves, we will find that wisdom will evade us in that particular area of our life. So, if you need to work on something, work on it. If you need to do something, do it. If you need to say something, say it.

The desire to win at living your life as a Proverbs 31 Woman is wrapped in your ability to become discipline, while exercising self-control will keep your emotions from running on high; especially when making wise decisions. As you very well know, wisdom is priceless.

We cannot go wrong using practical wisdom. And, trust me; when all else fails, wisdom will not! Wisdom is available to us at all times, but it will not wait for us. Wisdom is definitely not intelligence; it is our ability to exercise good judgment without allowing our emotions to rule over us. There is no possible way to have all the answers. Simply exercise wisdom and common sense when answering questions or discussing issues that provoke chaos and confusion. There are times when it is better not to say anything; and, trust me; this will win a debate every time. Oh, by the way, it only takes a fraction of a second to think before you speak, or to think before you react. Today, don't run from wisdom, run toward it, and watch the doors of understanding swing wide open.

Her Virtue
Her virtue came from her strength of character; she was not a superwoman. She knew the value of balance and having a system in place without worrying about people, places, and things that did not have a bearing on what she was doing, saying, or becoming. She was the keeper of her home and a keeper of herself. She learned the value of taking care of herself to ensure that she was able to show hospitality to others. And, not only that, she exuded a lot of Christ-like Breadcrumbs:

She has harmony from within.
She is very balanced.

She exudes courage.
She is gracious.
She is kind.
She is generous.
She is happy.
She is unselfish.
She is organized.
She is clean.
She exudes inner beauty.
She is wise.

The Proverbs 31 Woman's **#1 Breadcrumb** of all time, is......, are you ready for this......it is **Time-Management**. In order to gain control over our lives, we must find a way to plan our day to control our time. Of course, creating a to-do list will help, but there is much more to time management. We must also have a not-to-do list to better govern our time. This will ensure that our time is not wasted on unproductive or unfruitful people, places, and things that contradict the core value of what we are trying to accomplish. Of course, there will be some things that we cannot control, but for the most part, we need to become a good steward of the time in which we do have.

Our time has a secret element of power, keeping us in control even when we are pushed to the limit. When we try to manage our time or when we are pushed to the limit, we must also make an attempt to maximize the time in which we do have. When life requires more time than we are willing to give, if we do not have a plan, we will find ourselves turning around to retreat back to the familiar. This is the point where most people give up or get lost in the issues of life. As we may very well know, we become what we think about, and we think about what we are becoming. So, why do we think that we never have enough time, when time is on our side? Of course, we will juggle things from time-to-time; but if we lose ourselves in the midst of the juggle then that becomes an issue. When we put the big and the little things into its proper perspective, we will find that the things that we feel are important are not and vice-versa.

If you plan your day before it starts, it will definitely give you a jump-start on your day when you get up in the morning. You will be surprised at how much time you will save by simply planning. In order to gain control over your life you must:

- *Know why this goal is important to you.*

- *Know what type of impact it's going to have on your life.* Anything worth having, we are going to sacrifice something, and it's up to you to know what that something is.

- *Keep your goals simple but not easy.* Life is not hard; therefore, goals are not hard—it is our power of choice or being pushed out of our comfort zone that becomes difficult. In so many words, our thoughts are really what keep things complicated in our life. However, the more you become accustomed to setting and achieving your goals; you will become a pro at it.

- *Think about your goals thoroughly and visualize them.* We are very visual. If you cannot see mentally what you believe, then more than likely you will not get it. It's important to be able to see mentally what you desire to bring it into reality.

- *Make a plan on how you are going to get one step closer to your goal every day.*

- *Keep yourself organized.* Clutter cause distractions mentally; therefore, affecting the flow of your process of thought.

- *Read your goals 6 days a week and take 1 day off.* It's imperative that you read your goals over and over—this will definitely help keep you on track. This is actually adjusting your thoughts to accommodate what you desire from your goal, passion, or dream.

- *Pray about it.* This keeps you sincere, and it keeps you on the right road, even if you come to some form of crossroad in your life. You must know that God is your source that will provide the resources necessary to accomplish your goal, passion, or dream.

- *Keep your goals achievable*—take one step at a time to ensure that you do not become overwhelmed.

- *Align yourself in the environment of your goal.*

- *Get a support group, mentor, or coach.* Support from others keeps you more committed to your goal. It's easy to hide the accomplishment of a goal if it's kept a secret; but if your goal is made known to others, you are not going to give up as easily. Plus, it's always good to have a coach or mentor.

- *Maximize all of your resources.* A goal is not set in stone; therefore, we don't know which stone will provide an added benefit. And, for that reason, we must not leave any stone unturned when working toward a goal. We must utilize all of our resources.

- *Focus on the goal and not your past failures or mishaps.* Keep a positive mindset at all times. Keep an accurate evaluation of where you are or how close you are to your goal.

- *Set a deadline or timeline for yourself.* This will better help you get to your desired destination in a timely manner.

- *Now, it's time to take action.* If you fail at taking action one day, take action the next day without giving up on yourself.

- *We must keep an open mind to ensure that we are able to recognize opportunity* when it presents itself in our life without becoming obsessed with it.

- *Journal every day.* This will help you keep track of what you are doing, and the reasons why. Don't forget to journal about your King.

These are some ways to help you better govern your time and how to preserve your virtue. And, don't forget to keep it positive at all cost.

Dealing with People

People are going to reject a Proverb's 31 Woman, just because they want to. As a Virtuous Woman, this should not change our attitude toward them at all. With anything in life, we are going to have the nay-sayers, and this is where our virtuosity is exuded. Therefore, you must keep it positive and don't waste too much time trying to convince anyone that you a Proverb's 31 Woman or a Virtuous Woman. It is not necessary to convince someone who has his or her mind already made up. Don't be afraid to move on to someone who will give you an opportunity to share what you have to offer. When you know that you have value in yourself, don't waste it on those who spend time devaluing people, places, and things that are providing a good service to those who need it. When all else fails, a winning attitude will not!

Stay on top of your game

My Virtuous Woman, if you want to stay on top of your game, you must prepare to do so. Preparation prevents us from making excuses for idling when we should be propelling forward. We spend more time trying to figure out how to avoid people, places, and things in our lives opposed to preparing ourselves for the great unknown. We often limit ourselves by the way we make excuses for not reaching beyond our comfort zone. Living our lives in fast forward can, and will cause us to jump from one thing to the next. And, jumping into things without preparing ourselves or thinking about what we are doing causes the best of us to make simple mistakes that could or should have been avoided. Of course, we will not be able to prepare for everything; but, we can prepare for some things.

Chapter 17

From the Bored Room

We often look at Delilah as a negative character in the Bible; however, she left us some valuable Breadcrumbs behind. Of course, we all know that she seduced and betrayed Sampson; but, what we don't realize is that Sampson allowed her to seduce and deceive him. How do I know? Judges 16 says that he tricked her several times before he told her the truth! That means—he knew what she was up to. Sampson is partially responsible for what happened to him because he had ample opportunity to walk away—he chose not to. Plus, he took his gift for granted—he knew that he was sleeping with the enemy! However, Delilah had a virtue that he was not able to find in any other woman, including his wife that betrayed him by telling his secret to a riddle, and was given away to his best-man as a wife; which was a big hit below the belt, and a blow to the ego for Samson that set him on a rampage. Maybe, he was still grieving over that—who knows.

And, I will tell you why—Delilah possessed something that he was not able to find in any other woman. Delilah did not allow him to get away with being evasive as he did with other women. She was able to get him to communicate with her, and that is how she was able to seduce him, mentally. Even though she used her seduction in the wrong way, this is where we can understand her mistake or her waywardness. However, instead of doing the wrong thing like Delilah did, I am going to show you how to use her Breadcrumbs to do the right thing to bring about a blessing.

My Virtuous Woman, we often look at seduction in a negative way; however, it becomes very positive when it's understood and used properly. Just to let you know, all women are born with some form of seduction—it may go unnoticed; however, it's there! Often enough, we as women are only focused on seducing a man physically; and, that is not the proper way of doing so. Never seduce a man into committing to you—this is a recipe for disaster. Seduction gets old when a man does not have the proper emotional support to sustain a seduced commitment. If you desire to have a man to become your King, you must seduce him mentally. You must be able to stimulate his mind, first; while stimulating his emotions, secondly.

As a Virtuous Woman, we must understand that Delilah was:

1. Spontaneous.
2. Clever.
3. Sensual.
4. Wise.
5. Attractive.
6. Well-mannered.
7. Presumptuous.

The most important Breadcrumb of the downfall of Sampson—Delilah was the only woman that was able to get him to laugh. She brought joy to his heart. When you can get a man to laugh in your arms, it is really easy to get his heart! That is one Breadcrumb that you will never want to forget—laughter is indeed medicine for the weary soul.

Sampson was hurting, he was tired, he was always fighting, he was always on the defense, and he was always on guard; but, when it came to Delilah—he rested. At that moment, he rested his head in the wrong place—there are times when the strong, gets weak, if they are wounded bad enough, if a wound has not healed, they will rest their heads in the lap of the enemy, only to have their strength taken away from them—just for being human! However, she did all the right things for the wrong reasons. On one hand, she gave him peace, and on the other hand, she ensnared him—this is not the way to use our Virtue.

We do not have to play manipulative games with our King to get what we want, or to ensnare him. My Virtuous Woman, it's hard to sugar-coat our credibility once it's lost—after this incident, Delilah lost her credibility with those who respected her sensual beauty. Of course, we can become known for what we want to be known for; yet, once our credibility is lost, it is hard to regain. As we all know, a good name is chosen. However, the need to be accepted will cause us to sacrifice our credibility for the temporary comfort of having a seemingly good name or reputation. We need to exercise caution when sugar-coating our reality—if we lose our integrity or credibility, what's the probability of having a good name or reputation? Good question and we all know that it is highly improbable. My Virtuous Woman, our credibility is one characteristic that we do not want to lose.

Chapter 18

Her Excellency

Her Excellency is a Virtuous Woman that's designed to excel; and, the fluidity of a Virtuous Woman is surrounded by excellence. Even though a Virtuous Woman is not perfect, she has a sincere desire to be perfected knowing that she is a work in progress.

The first rule of thumb is not to get our goals mixed up with our purpose. Our purpose gives us the meaning or reason for doing what we do; however, setting goals will give us something to work toward or give us something to work at. As a matter of fact, we must have some sort of way to measure our progress. Utilizing the positive impact of learning will prevent our growth from becoming stunted. We are designed to learn, grow, and become more than what we are today. My Virtuous Woman, we all want to become successful at something whether we admit to it or not. Now, in order for us to become successful at something, we must learn. Learning more is not always a common practice for everyone. The individuals who tend to refuse to learn more of what they don't know will eventually become closed-minded to change. In so many words, they will start resisting change, when change is inevitable. When you positively think through, strategize, prioritize, and learn, there is no limit on what you can achieve. As a matter of fact, that's a powerful combination that will have a lasting effect on you as well as those around you.

Structure helps us to streamline our ability to persist at things that pose some form of resistance. Structure is well needed in our lives, especially when it comes down to knowing what we don't want and what we do. My Virtuous Woman, having structure in our lives will help us to think about things before we take action. Of course, we will not be able to please everyone 100% of the time, we will not be right 100% of the time, nor will we be wrong 100% of the time; but, we can exercise our integrity 100% of the time. However, when we have structure backed by our integrity we are better equipped to overcome the resistant places in our lives.

My Virtuous Woman, why stress ourselves out over people, places, and things, when structure is designed to put them into the proper perspective. Just remember, people, places, and things come into your life for a reason, and they will also exit your life for a reason as well. With that being said, I want you to maximize every moment, taking what you need from life, and discarding the rest. When it comes down to the structure that you have in your life, what's going on outside of you is just as important as what's going on inside of you. So, take a minute to evaluate what you allow into your space and what you are going to get rid of, because your King is waiting for you.

Compromising No-No's

My Virtuous Woman, there may come a time in your life when you may become faced with a compromising situation. The story about Bathsheba always comes to mind when I think about a woman that allowed herself to be put in a compromising situation. Her story was a story of seduction, betrayal, and responsibility.

Bathsheba was the wife of Uriah, who went off to battle. In Bathsheba's time of loneliness, she was invited to the house of King David. She accepted the invitation out of obligation, after David sat, and watched her bathe from the top of his house. Even though David abused his authority to seduce Bathsheba, she did put herself in the situation, and she did consent to have relations with him. However, they did not expect for her to become pregnant. In order for David to cover up their actions, he plotted the death of Bathsheba's husband, and then married her.

Have you ever had an overwhelming desire for something that was strictly forbidden? Did the desire consume your every thought? My Virtuous Woman, there is temptation in every woman, and there is temptation in every man; however, the difference is that we must not allow ourselves to become enticed with the entertainment of the forbidden fruit. Yes, you may appear strong, but if you are constantly entertaining the thought of the temptation—it may cause you to fall short in your time of weakness.

David was a man after God's own heart, and he fell short in the area that he entertained. Now, if there is some form of temptation that has the potential to cause you to suffer great loss—do not, and I mean do not, put yourself in a position to become tempted or put yourself in a position to become defiled. Sometimes, you can't even entertain certain conversation with certain people, because it is so easy to have an affair without having sex. Secret meeting such as lunches, dinners, movies, vacations, etc. with a person of the opposite sex without the knowledge of your spouse opens the door of temptation. If you have to hide something like this from your spouse, something is definitely wrong, and you need to reevaluate your intentions. Just entertaining such issues and thoughts lay the foundation for an affair to occur in the mind. Yes, you are a strong woman; but, you are human! We do make mistakes and for that reason, here are some Breadcrumbs to flee temptation to protect your Virtuous Womanship:

1. Trust yourself to do the right thing.
2. Know and understand what you are feeling and why?
3. Make sure you are doing it for you and no one else.
4. Avoid sexually explicit conversations.
5. Watch out for the intimate touching or feeling.
6. Guard your heart.
7. Don't go near a place you know that will entertain your weakness.
8. Don't consume your mind with lustful or perverted thoughts. Replace those thoughts with something constructive and positive.
9. Focus on your self-control from the inside out, not the outside in.
10. Keep yourself active and busy.
11. Pray.

Bathsheba knew that she made a mistake, and she accepted responsibility for her actions. After doing so, she accepted the loss of her child; and, she picked up the pieces of her life to move forward with a legacy of wisdom for other Virtuous Women like you. As a matter of fact, her legacy tells us that if we have fallen short or someone else has fallen short here are some Breadcrumbs:

1. Do not become emotional about it.
2. Do not become anxious.
3. Do not become a victim of circumstance.
4. Do not become confrontational.
5. Do not gossip about your ordeal with your friends.
6. Do not make rash decisions.
7. Do not continue to badger the cheater about his or her mistake.
8. Do not become a cheater yourself.
9. Do not go through his or her stuff.
10. Do know what you want and what you will not tolerate.
11. Do remember that everything is not about you.
12. Do acknowledge God and allow Him to direct your path.
13. Do look within self, regarding why your partner cheated
14. Do understand why you attracted him or her in your life.
15. Do look at the big picture of why the two of you came together.
16. Do forgive regardless of whether he or she is right or wrong.
17. Do communicate with the cheater.
18. Work it out if necessary or leave it alone.
19. Do understand that time will heal all wounds.
20. Do continue to walk in love.

My Virtuous Woman, regardless of what brought you and your King together, becoming too emotional will break you apart, if you choose not to resolve a situation or circumstance in the spirit of love. A relationship needs trust, love, commitment, forgiveness, honesty, and balance. When an affair is committed, there is an underlying issue that needs to be resolved. And, by opening up to your partner to tell them what's wrong may very well be a hard thing to do. Nevertheless, if you don't learn how to respond to the needs of your spouse, you may lose something or someone you love and cherish deeply. It is hard to continue to love someone who does not love you enough to stop cheating on you; and when that spouse leaves, then the shoulda, coulda, and woulda will not work anymore." Sometimes we don't realize how much of a good thing we have until it is gone.

Now, with that being said, despite the seductive affair, Bathsheba, later gave birth to Solomon, who was considered to be the wisest King. And, I am pretty sure, he learned some of that wisdom from the virtue of his mother.

Chapter 19
The Cry

We are all going to go through something, and when it's our time to go through, we must keep our head up. The story of Hannah is a prime example of how to hold on to that little ray of hope. Hannah was the barren 2nd wife of Elkanah. Her feeling of barrenness overwhelmed her as she had to share her husband with another woman. Can you imagine sharing your husband with another woman? Hannah's heart was crying out as Peninnah, the other wife of Elkanah, constantly picked on her because she was without child.

Hannah took her grief and prayed through it. She was faithful in her plea to God for a child. Hannah is the idea prayer warrior; she got in God's face and did not give up. Then, one day, God blessed her with a child. Not only did He give her a child, but He also gave her a prophet. Her son was well known as the Prophet Samuel, who anointed Saul, and David as King.

Hannah's Breadcrumbs of Virtue:

1. Ask God for faith.
2. Be willing to receive it.
3. Submit to being molded into His perfection.
4. Be humble and obedient.
5. Acknowledge God's presence in your life.
6. Know that God is your protector.
7. Ask for total guidance.
8. Think of success and not failure.
9. Give thanks in all things.
10. Be patient.
11. Speak success.
12. Believe in yourself.
13. Think big thoughts and ideas.
14. Think and speak positively.
15. Keep track of your stepping-stones and lessons.
16. Never let go of your faith. Faith will carry you through when nothing else will.
17. Ask for what you want.
18. Get in the environment of your wants and needs.
19. Don't quit. You may lack money, time, and energy but never faith.
20. Be willing to receive help; you may not be able to do everything by yourself. Just don't depend on or believe in someone else. You must believe in God to lead your every footstep.
21. Try new things—get out of your comfort zone.

My Virtuous Woman, prayer changes things. The secret behind Hannah's prayers is that she gave her son back to God. When God blesses you with what you have been praying for, activate the law of reciprocity and give it back to Him. Meaning, if you give what you have to the Divine Will of God, He will bless it to be a blessing to others.

The moral of the story is, once you enter into your Virtuous Womanship, you must help or motivate others through your blessing, regardless of what other issues that you may have to deal with.

Keep Your Breadcrumb Exciting

A Virtuous Woman enjoys having fun with herself, her King, her family, and friends. She is a natural entertainer. When we are having fun at what we do, we have much less time to become stressed out over things that may work against us. As a matter of fact, stressed out people are usually the most worried people. Worrying about people, places, and things can and will put pressure on us and usually when we are under pressure, we overdo it, and chase people away. For that reason, we must exercise kindness at all times, regardless of how we may feel.

The Shunammite woman believed in entertaining the prophets, and she used her kindness, and wealth as a Breadcrumb to do so. This well respected, wealthy woman leaves behind valuable information for Virtuous Women on how to be content, kind, and persistent. However, kindness is sometimes mistaken as a weakness; yet, a kind word, along with a kind heart makes you invaluable. Kindness does not mean that you allow someone to walk all over you; kindness does mean that you possess the strength and the confidence to control your emotions regardless of the situation or circumstance. Kindness can melt away anxiety and build up confidence. Genuine kindness has such an impact on the human heart that it can turn a negative situation into something positive. As a matter of fact, it will take you places that cruelty and selfishness will never take you. Love and respect the kindness that's within you and kindness will reward you with great strength, confidence and the effectiveness that is needed to keep you blessed. Oh, by the way, kindness is contagious, and our quality of life is best revealed in how we nurture our relationship with ourselves and others.

Chapter 20

Rubies From Within

Wisdom can be applied to enhance and improve the quality of your life. A wise Virtuous Woman must think like an attorney; she must think objectively, independently, and concisely while allowing the Holy Spirit to govern her from within. My Virtuous Woman, wisdom is a viable asset needed to prevent you from over-thinking, rationalizing, or justifying what's in black and white.

Wisdom is a commonly overlooked birthright because we often try to make sense of things that are not designed for us to understand. However, once we understand the value of wisdom, it will always give us the opportunity to take action, solve problems, and to make decisions pertaining to our goals or ambitions. Not only that, but wisdom will also nudge us when not to make a decision as well. It has a way of causing us to look deep within to find the hidden knowledge about things that we may have buried or the things that we are choosing not to deal with. We all have some smarts about us, but wisdom gives us the opportunity to think differently than those who are going simply on natural knowledge.

Successful abundance is at its best when we make the necessary adjustments in our action plan to reach our maximum potential. Continuing to do the same thing, expecting a different result is not wise. We need to change things up from time-to-time in order to reach our maximum potential. And, by doing so, there is no need to waste time and energy on something that's not working or something that's bringing about defeat. In order to successfully create abundance in our lives, we must spend more time and energy changing our approach to why people, places, and things are not working. Once we analyze our approach, we are better able to determine the necessary changes.

Choices are a part of life, when we do not make wise choices— it becomes quite evident. Of course, we are not able to fix everything, but we can determine why something is not working, and make some adjustments if need be. My Virtuous Woman, this is where our flexibility is established. There are going to be times when we need to change our plan of action; however, the recognition of the change is of great importance. We must recognize and commit to change before the change can actually take place. Changing something that we feel as if change is not necessary, creates a double-negative; therefore, making change or the transition very difficult.

When you want something bad enough, you will make the changes necessary to get what you want or get rid of what you don't want. Choices are not hard at all—they just require a commitment to know what you need, and what you don't need in your life. My Virtuous Woman, even if you are having a difficult time with change, prayer will change things. And, regardless of where you are right now in your prayer life, simply ask for help. It is one of the most effective tools used in the process of change; yet, it is the most overlooked, and the most misunderstood! Today, embrace the essence of your change to ensure that your life becomes a representation of wise choices.

Chapter 21
Diligence

When a Virtuous Woman assumes her role, she becomes very diligent in what she does. She understands that laziness and slothfulness are not going to strengthen her touch with her King. A Virtuous Woman must keep herself busy, but well-balanced.

We must be active; when we are not active, we will tend to expect our King to give us more attention than we really need. Lazy women are the most depressed women. We must keep ourselves busy with family, friends, activities, etc.; of course, with an equal balance of being available to our King.

Unproductive actions provide an impediment that will become hard for us to recognize once it becomes a habit. Unproductive actions can and will create a desire to have or get something for nothing. In everything that we do, say, or become will have a price tag attached to it, whether we recognize it or not.   Making excuses for our slothfulness will not help us become more productive. As a matter of fact, it makes room for unjustified impediments that contributes to the lack of discipline in certain areas of our lives. Pretending that we do not have enough time to devote to the people, places, and things we desire sets the pace for the results that we are receiving. Furthermore, the simple resistance of making a temporary sacrifice will cause us to eventually make some sort of permanent sacrifice. So, with that being said, we must count the cost in all things.

Fine-tuning our actions is a great way to overcome any unproductive actions that may temporarily work against us. Of course, the price of persistence is not going to be free—it's going to take work in order to get to the next level in life. Yes, we all want to be logical; but what do we do when our logic is not working? As we usher in our prosperity, we must find a way to make the sacrifices necessary to get what we want or to get rid of what we don't need. Of course, it may not be easy but with persistence and perseverance, we can do anything.

As a Virtuous Woman, you are blessed to be a blessing to someone else and not just a blessing to yourself—it's your responsibility to find a way to motivate someone through your wisdom, creativity, ambitions, or skills to ensure that you maximize the law of use. And, it's a shame to allow an unused or misused blessing to fall by the wayside. My Virtuous Woman, it's imperative that you count the cost of your thoughts, actions, and reactions to ensure that you are not sabotaging your own success or the success of your King. When you program your mind to succeed at whatever you desire to do, you gain more strength to get up when you fall short or to step down when something is not working for you or your Kingdom.

We can actually think about something for years, but if we do not put any action behind our thoughts, then what do we have? It's real simple; we have unplanned action. Just pay attention to the ant, they are constantly and consistently building. Thinking ahead of the game is great, but we must be willing to work toward what we think, and think about what we would like to work toward. When we think a thought, we must take into account the action that's needed to carry out that thought. There must be an equal balance between the two in order to keep our mind and eye coordination in sequence. As a matter of fact, when our time is full of clutter, we will lose track of it as soon as we become distracted. Our best bet is to form a to-do list and a not-to-do list. This will keep us from wasting time on people, places, and things that cause us to fall short where we should be standing tall for ourselves, our King, and our Kingdom.

Drifting aimlessly away from our goals is commonly the reason we create excuses not to do what needs to be done. Some people live their lives making excuses for not doing; some people make excuses for not living, and some people make excuses to live. Regardless of the excuse, it does not negate the fact that we must accept responsibility for our actions, reactions, commitments, and the lack thereof. When we become lazy mentally, we often cover it up by uneventful excuses that drive us away from our goal or commitments. You must find a way to center your actions on the goal and not the excuse. Your future is in your, and it's going to be up to you what you do with it. If you are in it to win, you will find that you will start making progress in the right direction until you cross the finish line of ultimate success. From me to you, if you are going to make an excuse—make an excuse to succeed!

A Systematic Ant

Most of your mental, physical, and emotional turmoil are due to spiritual deprivation. When the chains of turmoil weigh down your spirit, you will not be able to successfully carry out a balanced lifestyle. And no matter how you try to fool yourself into thinking that you are in control, your situations, and circumstances will speak for themselves. You will see that everything around you will start to get worse rather than better.   Listed below are five indications of a weighted down spirit:

1. Confused easily
2. Frustrated
3. Easily angered
4. Depressed
5. Controlling

A broken system creates rebellion. And, rebellion has a way of causing us to think that the rules of life do not apply to us. Take it from an ant; rules are not made to be broken; they are made to create boundaries to protect us in some way, shape, or form to create harmony in our colonized Kingdom. However, when we allow the secret act of rebellion to settle in our heart, we will find that we feel exempt from following the rules. When we pick and choose what we want to obey, we then place limits on ourselves and others without realizing it. When doing our own thing without having limits, we will find that rationalization will become our best friend. As we all know, we can justify and rationalize anything that we want or don't want as long as we are able to get our way. However, this is not always a good thing to do—it opens the door to many lame excuses, especially when we make a mess of our lives and create enemies. And, breaking all the rules to get what you want will not get you any brownie points when your Kingdom is at your disposal!

My Virtuous Woman, let me drop a little Breadcrumb of wisdom on you—rules actually teach you how to respect yourself as a Virtuous Woman, your man as a King, your family as an inheritance and others as a way of exercising your servitude; therefore, keeping you honest about the people, places, and things that can easily beset you.

Spring Cleaning

A Virtuous Woman places high value on keeping the cobwebs from invading her territory. Spring cleaning from within is an excellent way of getting rid of the cobwebs that may get us entangled in unpleasant things. When the battles are raging from within, a soulful cleaning from within will create a harmony that keeps us balanced temporarily until we encounter another challenge. Being that a soulful cleansing is only temporary, then what is it? A soulful cleaning consists of getting rid of negative thoughts, actions, and reactions through prayer, fasting, and meditation. This process does not take a lot of skill or talent; it starts with a DECISION—a decision to change our negative patterns into positive ones. As a matter of fact, when a Virtuous Woman makes a decision to get rid of clutter, it's her way of symbolically making room for her blessings as she cleans the corners of her heart as well.

The power of our forgiveness can be used as superglue to mend the bridge of a broken relationship or friendship that would not otherwise come back together. As we do our spring cleaning, we are cleaning the house on our brokenness as well. And, of course, we have all suffered a broken heart at least once in our life, some more than others; however, we somehow healed, right? May be or may be not; but, if we are still holding a grudge, any form of resentment, any form of anger, etc.—we have not Healed.

Forgiveness has a form of adhesive that will heal or mend seemingly irreparable brokenness. It has been proven that we remember the bad more than we remember the good. Of course, it's not that we want to, it's human nature. My friend, someone can have 100 acts of kindness and 1 act that we do not agree with, we will remember the 1 act that has caused us pain, opposed to the 100 acts that we were able to benefit from. For this reason, when things seem bad, we must force ourselves to look for the GOOD.

Brokenness can teach us, and it can also hinder us from living a fulfilled life. My friend, crying over a wounded heart for 10, 20 or 30 years is a long time to wallow in hurt, and this is exactly how a caring and loving heart can become a heart of stone. Stone-cold love hurts! Not only does it hurt the stone-cold person, but it also hurts the people that he or she may come in contact with on a daily basis. My Virtuous Woman, a stone-cold person, creates a domino effect of stone-cold people without realizing that they have contributed to their own circle of continual hurt. When it comes down to the matters of the heart, we don't want to talk about it. But, in order to enjoy the fruits of your labor, you must check the consistency of your heart to ensure that it does not become a heart of stone. My Virtuous Woman, it's imperative that we live and love while laughing our way to the Virtuous Womanship—this is as it should be.

Chapter 22

The Law of Reciprocity

The virtue of a woman is empowered by her strength. However, strength without morals has led up to women becoming overly controlling, and too strong for their own good. My Virtuous Woman, your virtue lies in your ability to exude courage topped off with moral excellence. Once this is done, your vitality of greatness will soon polish off your ethical principles of your Virtuous Womanship status; therefore, keeping what's going on in your house out of the streets. A phenomenal Virtuous Woman understands her virtue and does not allow others to sift her Kingdom based on their opinions. Her Kingdom is run on her ability to walk upright and steadfast, keeping everything in its proper perspective. She's not the type of woman that would tear her house down with her bare hands; instead, she builds her house on the principle of "one hand washes the other." With her graceful influence, she builds her home into a castle of substance and love.

This is my last story about Sarah, the wife of Abraham, the Mother of Isaac; she too was a Virtuous Woman. She is by far my favorite of them all—she stood behind Abraham at all cost, and God stood behind her decisions as well; especially when God says to Abraham, *"In all that Sarah hath said unto thee, hearken unto her voice"* Gen 21:12. That says a lot when God respects the woman of the house; she has some serious Virtue tied up in that relationship. This woman was very wise, and it is obvious that Abraham sought her for counsel and guidance on certain things. Also, when God shuts down a Kingdom to pull **ONE** woman out, she is **SPECIAL**. He did that for 2 women that I know of in the Book of Genesis, and that was Sarah, Abraham's Wife; and, Rebekah, her son Isaac's wife. Although it was not mentioned, Abraham was not leading his people alone, Sarah was indeed leading in the background—they were a team, God knew it, Abraham knew it, and Sarah knew it.

Nevertheless, Sarah was getting older, and she wanted a family, and being a typical woman allowed her emotions to get in the way. She was probably more ashamed of being old and barren than anything else; but, anyway, she tried to force God's hand to create in her eyes a so-called blessing—opposed to allowing God to fulfill his promised to Abraham. Was Sarah trying to play God? Absolutely! Did God allow her? Absolutely? Why? To teach her a lesson. Why? Did she need to learn? God knew that she would come back to Him to get her out of that mess. When we lose trust and lack faith in God, that is what happens. When we trust God to take care of us, that's what He will do, and when we don't trust him, then we try to take care of our situation, and we do the best we can; and sometimes our best may or may not be good enough. Therefore, we have to go humbly back to the Source with our tail in between our legs. Okay, let's get back on track.

Sarah, playing God, went to the extreme of allowing her husband to sleep with her maid, Hagar, in order to have an heir to the throne due to her barrenness. Hagar, played her like a little fiddle—she thought Hagar was just going to hand over her child just like that—well, Sarah had another thing coming. Hagar had a plan of her own. In my opinion, Sarah created a mess; but, God Almighty can work around any mess that we make—that is why it is always good to exercise wisdom and patience in all things. When Hagar gave birth to Ishmael, she thought that she could take the place of Sarah in Abraham's heart. Low and behold, she was wrong.

Sarah may have had her moment; but, she was not stupid. That was a one-time deal—Hagar may have an heir to the throne; but, she was still her maid. Ishmael was an arrangement, and Sarah swallowed her pride for the purpose; but, when she came to herself, she began to deal harshly with Hagar. Just because, a person is limited in one area, doesn't mean that they have to bow down to the one that they are relying on for help—it could have been a win-win situation for Hagar and Sarah. But, for some odd reason, Hagar tried to play on Sarah's weakness, and Sarah had to bring her back down to earth. Sarah opened the front door of Virtue for Hagar—yet, her Slave Mentality got it closed right in her face, so she sent Hagar and Ishmael packing. Hagar and her son, Ishmael could have had a peace of the promise, but Hagar's slave mentality only got Ishmael a piece of his birthright; however, God was with him, and still blessed him anyway.

God finally blessed Sarah and Abraham with a son named Isaac, which received all of his Birthrights. In my opinion, Sarah, Abraham, and Hagar, they all share responsibility for their wrongdoing in this story; but in the end, somehow they all got back on track.

Sharing is the creative force that enhances the flow of positive change within you, and your environment without you having to sell yourself short. The act of sharing goes beyond just giving. Sharing is indeed a form of giving; but it has a little more care, thought, and emotions added to it. Regardless of whether a person is on the sharing or receiving end, we are blessed with the ability to govern our natural instincts of sharing. So, for all of the Virtuous Women out there, when it comes down to sharing your mate, exercise extreme caution—although Sarah had been with Abraham for a long time; and their relationship was solid as a rock. Hagar was able to put a dent in it that the GOD FEARING ALMIGHTY VIRTUOUS Sarah had to get beside herself, and get that home wrecking Hagar out of her house. There is a reason why I left this as the last story; I believe in sharing, Sarah believes in sharing, that is why she is one of the most Virtuous Woman of the Bible. Whenever there was a need Sarah was always sharing. When the Angel of the Lord, came to visit Abraham, and she got caught laughing, she was sharing then. That is also why her son, Isaac had to have a certain type of woman—she had to be the same Virtue. She was too sharing until she made a mistake and shared her man! And, Sarah had to get ugly. Real, Real, Ugly with Hagar! So, Ladies beware, when you share your house with another woman, make sure you make it known that your husband is off limits. If you have a maid, make it known that your husband is off limit; or get it in writing, contracts work really, really well. Take nothing for granted ladies, because if you do—I would say, that was your Hagar moment! Now, as I continue on with the rest of this chapter talking about sharing, I will be referring to other tangible things besides your mate.

It does not matter what we have, or what we do not have, hoarding out of lack or greed can, and will break the flow of our ability to share and receive. We are not born with the ability to hoard; it is developed during childhood, from a tragic event or some sort of conditioning. And, being that we are not born this way, positive change will always be within our reach to ensure that we are able to build, create, and enhance our lives as well as the lives of others. One of the best ways to receive the best of what God has for us is to share what we have. As we continue to grow, the natural instincts of sharing will move us regarding the right time to share as well as the right time to receive. The law of reciprocity stands regardless of who we are, our situation, our circumstance, or what we are going through—we are all able to share our Breadcrumbs, no matter what!

Your hidden treasure is in your Breadcrumb, trust it; believe in it; share it, and watch how it comes back to you in full circle. It's just sitting there waiting for you to share it with the world, and once you do that, everything else will work itself out. My Virtuous Woman, focus on the sharing and receiving aspect of your life to ensure that you are not breaking the flow of your natural resources, and watch how your Breadcrumbs will begin to work for you naturally, making your little, become much. From me to you, never underestimate the **Power of a Breadcrumb**, because this is mine. Be Blessed and Be a Blessing to Someone Else.

Virtuous Womanship
Index

About Him:

1. Listen to him without judging him. Try to reframe from offering your opinion until it's asked for—just sympathize and relate.

2. Don't try the change him! Your goal is to understand where he's coming from, where he's at and where he's going. This may require you to polish up those listening skills.

3. Get rid of the selfish agenda. You are going to have to find the need in this man instead of your wants and offer him a benefit with a sense of urgency with no strings attached.

4. Do your homework. He wants you to think about how you can serve as a benefit instead of a liability creating lasting value that's hard to replace.

5. Allow him to experience a sense of freedom.

6. Always let him know that he has options and that you value his wants and needs. This is a part of your priority in a relationship.

7. You must consider this man's feelings regarding everything you do.

8. No Drama. Patience will keep you from over-reacting to things you don't like.

9. Communication! You are going to have to communicate with this man in his language. Your job is to find what stimulates this man in a conversation that causes him to listen to you on any level.

10. Allow him to express himself, first. While maintaining eye contact if possible, giving a slight nod from time-to-time, confirming that you are listening to him.

11. Never expect him to carry your baggage from previous relationships. There are some things that you may have to expose out of honesty; but, there are some things that you are going to have to leave in the closet and vow to never expose them. Everyone has a past, but you never allow your past to prevent you from embracing your future.

12. Never expect him to be something that he's not.

13. Understand that he will make mistakes.

14. Discuss your likes, dislikes, fears, frustrations and expectations of each other to ensure that there will not be any surprises later on.

15. Try not to outright confront him when you catch him in a lie.

16. Try not to become confrontational.

17. He is not your child; so don't treat him like one.

18. Try not to make excuses for his shortcomings, express your concerns without arguing, screaming, fussing or fighting.

19. Understand that men have a different genetic makeup than you.

20. Men will not be driven by the same emotions that you will be—don't expect him to understand you if you are not sure you understand yourself.

21. Men are VISUAL. Take care of yourself. Don't let yourself go!

22. Don't try to read his mind—you might read it wrong. Ask fact-finding question always in the "I" form and never in the "You" form.

23. Let them know that you need them—Who wants to feel unneeded?

24. Allow him to tell you where he is emotionally able to deal with a relationship and whether he's attracted to you. This is when you will have to listen closely!

25. Make sure you do not use the past to prey upon his insecurities.

26. Relax and don't try to figure him out—you may figure wrong.

27. Help bring fulfillment into his life and not codependency. Your goal is to become interdependent and involved in his

life naturally. You don't have to force things to happen if it is for you—it will happen!

28. Let what happen in the past, stay in the past. Rehashing issues will not produce a pretty outcome.

29. Respect his space and never show up unannounced.

30. Value your privacy. People will deplete you of all your energy if you allow them to.

31. Guard your thoughts. Your thoughts create your reality.

32. Focus on the wants and not the DON'T WANTS.

33. Be cautious about where you get your information.

34. Exercise caution regarding who you allow into your life.

35. Know that your potential can cause the actual.

36. Consider yourself blessed at all times.

37. Never be afraid to say goodbye to the past and hello to your future every day.

38. Understand that you have been chosen for your own unique assignment.

39. Plan your life to create a wall of success.

About You:

1. Know what you want and want what you know.

2. Always remember that you are the "Virtuous Woman of your Crop." Just as the cream always rises to the top, so does the Virtuous Woman.

3. Never expect a relationship to make you happy.

4. Never compromise to satisfy an urge of temporary happiness.

5. You must be happy prior to going into a relationship with someone. If you are not, being miserable will become your middle name. You cannot expect anyone to do what you are not willing to do for yourself.

6. Don't appear so desperate or weak! Desperation makes you an EASY catch for trash.

7. Exercise being balanced with a hence of wise, pleasant vulnerability is key.

8. You must know that you are not incomplete without him.

9. Make sure you never beg for love. This will have to come naturally, he either feel it for your or he doesn't.

10. Clingy women usually suffocate men.   Men need space!

11. Maximize your sex appeal—be sexy.   Exude sexiness to create your own niche.

12. If he is always trying to get you in the bedroom, it does not take long to figure out what your relationship is based upon.   A relationship is doomed if it's just confined to the bedroom.

13. Stop playing Games with men—that's childish!

14. Express your feelings discreetly—if he reciprocates fine, if he doesn't, that's fine as well.

15. A man already has an idea of what he wants from you and how to get it.   Now it's up to you to know what it is.   No more excuses about he doesn't know what he wants—He does.   Most often, this is a sign that he's UNAVAILABLE, but he wants to be greedy for the fear of losing out!

16. Do not sacrifice your integrity to stay with him!

17. Make sure he is able to help you in your time of need.

18. Make sure that he treats you with respect.

19. Bring more to the table than just your body.   Men want a well-rounded woman.

20. If he does not want you—MOVE ON! Law of detachment.

21. No begging! Communicate yes, there is no need to beg.

22. Prevent yourself from trying to make up for what he is lacking.

23. If you have a gut feeling that something's wrong, it probably is. Don't Rush.

24. Always know that your soul mate is waiting for you.

25. Use your body language in a positive, sensual way to flirt with him. SECRET: Men like for women to discreetly flirt with them.

26. Don't get uptight when things are not going the way you had expected. Things change, people grow up, and people grow apart. Such as life.

27. Make sure you understand that a man is WYSIWYG. If you can't accept how he is right now, don't fool yourself into thinking that you can change him. God is the only one who can truly change an individual.

28. Don't let yourself go. The upkeep of your image is very important; I am not saying be consumed by your image but take care of your image.

29. Never lose your personal identity for a man. If you have to lose your identity for him, then he is not the one for you.

30. Take time to focus on the little things to attract his attention.

31. Make sure you don't crumble when he says something that you don't like or offend you.

32. Keep your mind active and don't over think issues or a relationship.

33. If a man leaves you for another woman, don't try to win him back or sabotage his relationship with someone else. Don't ignore the obvious signs, respectfully, MOVE ON. It may hurt to lose; your ego may be bruised; but trust me, it was only a matter of time before he moved on anyway. However, if it was meant to be, he will come back on his own.

34. Sharing him with another woman is a quick way to set yourself up for hurt. If he is not ready to commit to you and you alone, then your best bet is to keep moving—being emotionally committed to two women at the same time is dangerous and unhealthy.

35. Keep yourself busy—there is no need to sit around waiting on a man when you can make your life more productive.

36. Actions speak louder than words.

37. Never let him see you sweat. Stay calm and don't freak out about the big or small things. Controlling your emotions will help you control your attitude and actions to enable you to deal with issues that tend to come out of nowhere.

38. Make time for you and your girlfriends, never neglect your girls 100% of the time to wait for him. Give yourself space to ensure that you have the freedom to socialize with others to keep you in touch with the world outside of him.

39. No insecurity, please. Never belittle yourself at all cost.

40. Don't call him too much unless that is what he requests.

41. Do not become codependent or go into a relationship with the intent of using someone for material gain-- Gold-digger. Get your own!

42. Always give him enough room to hang himself— whatever he's doing will come out, you don't have to look for it, pry or snoop.

43. If you want to see him, just make your request known.

44. Don't play childish games with him trying to win his heart.

45. Be a Virtuous Woman and your King will take his rightful place.

www.ingramcontent.com/pod-product-compliance
Lightning Source LLC
LaVergne TN
LVHW021505080426
835509LV00018B/2413